UNDERWATER BATTLES

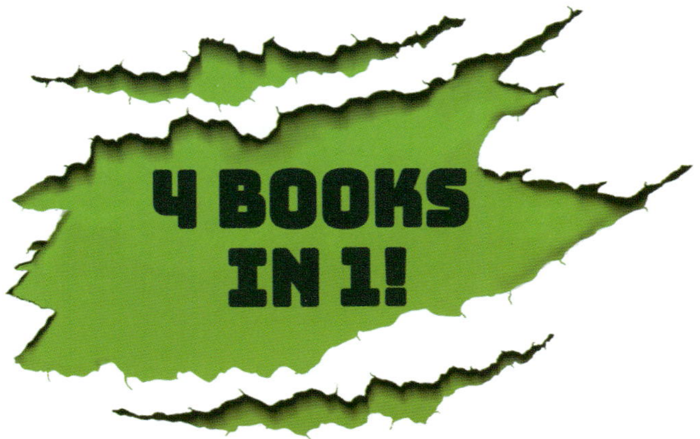

BY
JERRY
PALLOTTA

ILLUSTRATED BY
ROB
BOLSTER

SCHOLASTIC

The publisher would like to thank the following for their kind permission to use their photographs in this book:

Photos ©: 8: Norbert Wu/Superstock, Inc.; 9: Shane Gross/Shutterstock; 10: Chris Newbert/Minden Pictures; 11: WaterFrame/Alamy Stock Photo; 24 bottom: Azure Computer & Photo Srvs/Animals Animals; 25 top: Jez Tryner/BluePlanetArchive; 25 center: Doug Perrine/BluePlanetArchive; 25 bottom: Brandon Cole Marine Photography; 38 bottom: Courtesy of Skulls Unlimited; 39 bottom: Doc White/BluePlanetArchive; 44 bottom: pbpgalleries/Alamy Stock Photo; 45 bottom: geckophoto/Getty Images; 46: Brandon Cole Marine Photography; 47: Klein and Hubert/Minden Pictures; 52: Alaska Stock LLC/Alamy Stock Photo; 53: Brandon Cole Marine Photography; 75 top right: flySnow/Getty Images; 75 bottom right: Pigprox/Shutterstock; 79 crab pot: NOAA Central Library Historical Fisheries Collection; 82 top: Carol Perry Davis; 82 bottom: Dorset Media Service/Alamy Stock Photo; 83 bottom: Shari Romar; 87 top: Millard H. Sharp/Science Source; 104 bottom right: Dirk Renckhoff/Alamy Stock Photo; 108 center: akg-images/Newscom; 108 bottom: Chronicle/Alamy Stock Photo; 109: bullet74/Shutterstock; 111 bottom right: Louise Murray/Science Source; 116: Look and Learn/Bridgeman Images.

To cousin Jeanne Petronio, who comes from the hammerhead side of the family.
Thank you to my research assistants, Olivia Packenham and Will Harney.
To Bob, Betsy, and especially Christopher Detwiler.
This book is for Connie Ross, a New Hampshire reading legend.
—J.P.

To Eddie.
To Charlie, Eddie, Bobby D., and Teddy.
This book is dedicated to Edward Hopper.
—R.B.

ISBN 978-1-5461-5922-3

10 9 8 7 6 5 4 3 2 1 25 26 27 28 29

Printed in China 38

This edition first printing, 2025

-TABLE OF CONTENTS-

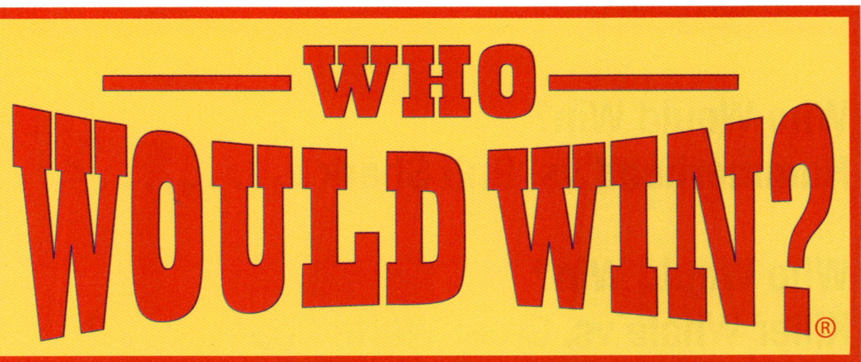
WHO
WOULD WIN?®

HAMMERHEAD
VS.
BULL
SHARK

What would happen if a hammerhead shark came face-to-face with a bull shark? What if they were both the same size? What if they were both hungry? If they had a fight, who do you think would win?

GREAT HAMMERHEAD SHARK

Its head has a strange shape.

MAKO SHARK

The fastest-swimming shark!

REMEMBER THIS!
Fish have gills, not lungs.

MEGAMOUTH SHARK

A recently discovered deepwater shark with a huge mouth.

BULL SHARK

This shark has attacked more people than any other shark.

WHALE SHARK

'he largest fish in the world. It is a harmless filter feeder.

GREAT WHITE SHARK

The famous movie star needs no introduction!

FACT
Sharks are saltwater fish.

TIGER SHARK

The "garbage can" of the sea. It eats almost everything.

SCIENTIFIC NAME OF GREAT HAMMERHEAD:
"Sphyrna mokarran"

Meet the great hammerhead. It can grow to be twenty feet long and can weigh one thousand pounds. Hammerhead sharks are easy to identify, because they have a head shaped like a hammer.

FUN FACT
Scientists call the hammer-shaped head a cephalofoil.

DID YOU KNOW?
The largest hammerheads have heads that are three feet wide eyeball to eyeball.

Hammerheads look scary, but they hardly ever attack humans.

SCIENTIFIC NAME OF BULL SHARK:
"Carcharhinus leucas"

Meet the bull shark. It got its name from its stocky shape and unpredictable behavior. It is an aggressive shark that lives in shallow water, preferring water less than one hundred feet deep. Female bull sharks grow to be twelve feet long and to weigh five hundred pounds.

INTERESTING FACT
Great white sharks often get blamed for bull shark attacks.

DID YOU KNOW?
Because they live in shallow waters, bull sharks are more dangerous to people than great white sharks or tiger sharks, which prefer deep waters.

Hammerheads hunt by themselves at night. During the day, they migrate in huge schools.

Bull sharks prefer to be alone.

BONUS FACT

Despite their solitary nature, bull sharks sometimes hunt in twos.

SHARK TRIVIA

The bull shark has many names: Zambezi shark, estuary shark, java shark, Fitzroy Creek shark, ground shark, Swan River whaler, cub shark, freshwater shark, and Lake Nicaragua shark.

TYPES OF HAMMERHEADS

FUN FACT

The funny-shaped head allows them to have more sensors. Hammerheads can smell better and sense fish better than other sharks.

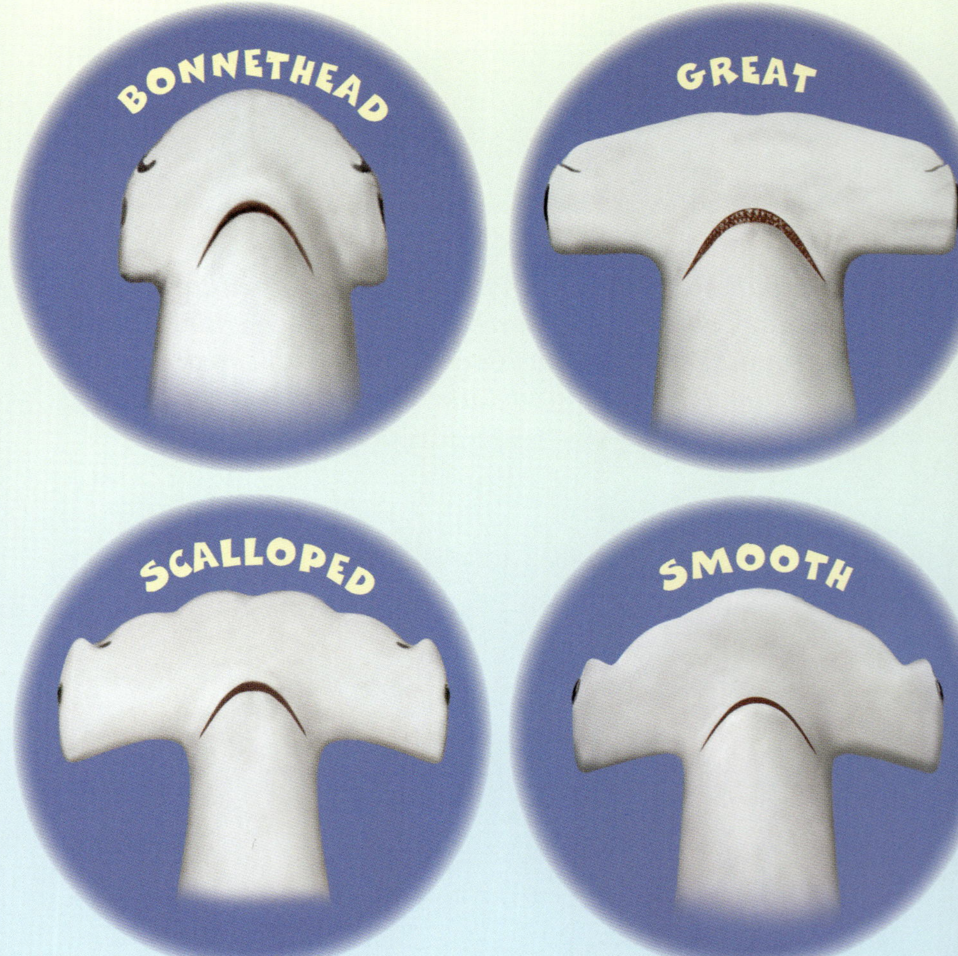

DID YOU KNOW?

Some other hammerhead species are the scoophead, golden hammerhead, whitefin hammerhead, winghead shark, and scalloped bonnethead.

BULL SHARK TRAVELS

ull sharks swim in shallow coastal water. They often wim into estuaries and up freshwater rivers.

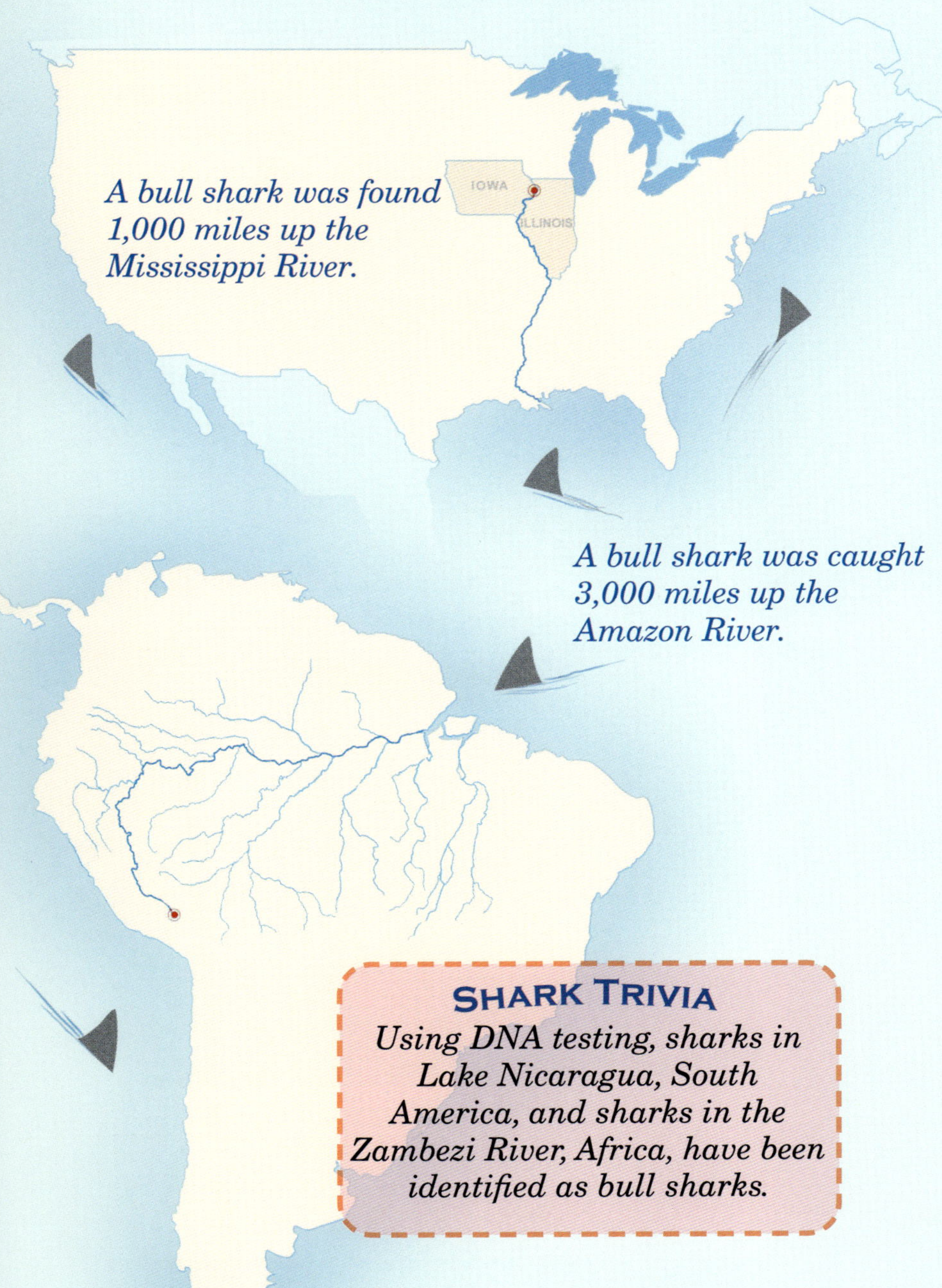

IOWA
ILLINOIS
A bull shark was found 1,000 miles up the Mississippi River.
A bull shark was caught 3,000 miles up the Amazon River.

SHARK TRIVIA

Using DNA testing, sharks in Lake Nicaragua, South America, and sharks in the Zambezi River, Africa, have been identified as bull sharks.

If you were scuba diving and a hammerhead swam at you this is what it would look like.

INTERESTING FACT

Hammerheads have swum in Earth's oceans for more than 20 million years.

DID YOU KNOW?

The unusual location of hammerheads' eyes allow them to see above, below, and all around!

you were skin diving and a bull shark swam right at you, his is what you would see. Yikes!

Fun Fact

Bull sharks' heads are wider than they are long.

Did You Know?

Bull sharks are known for bumping their prey first. After the bump, they decide if they want to bite.

HAMMERHEAD TOOTH

Compared to other sharks, hammerheads have small mouths. But hammerheads, like all sharks, have scary-looking teeth!

TIGER SHARK

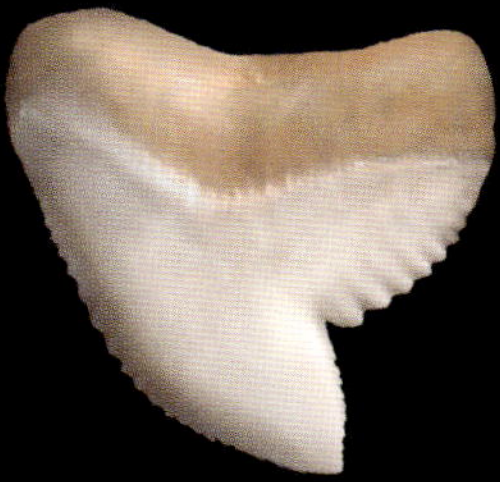

LEMON SHARK

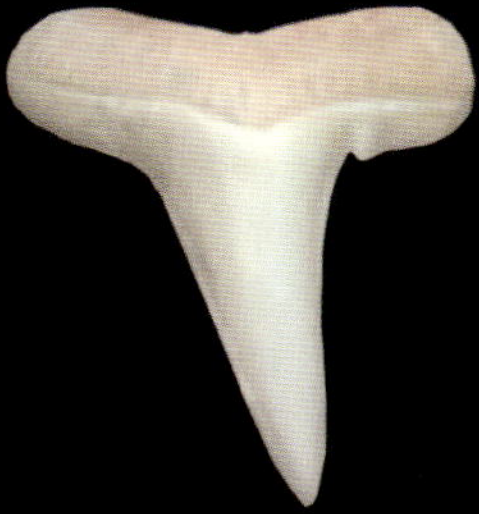

MAKO SHARK

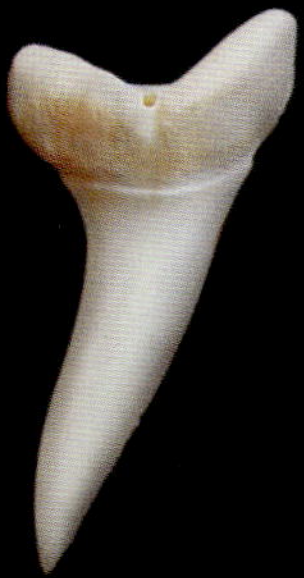

NURSE SHARK

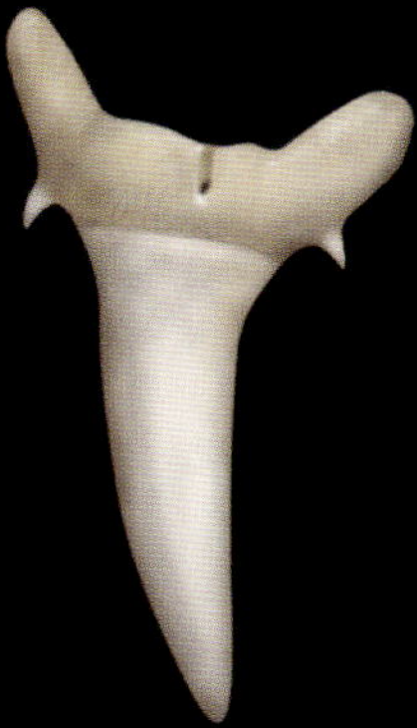

THRESHER SHARK

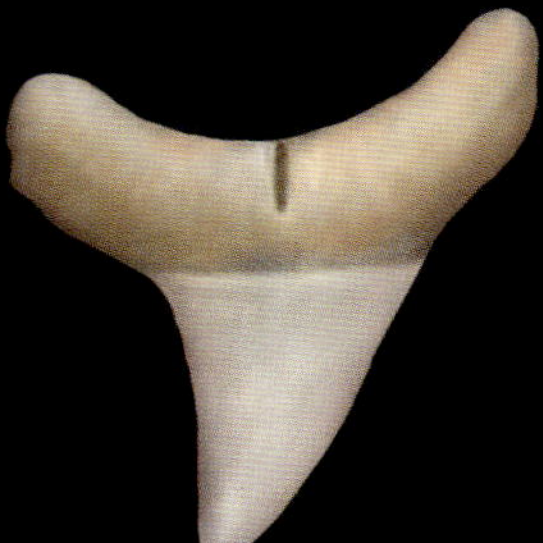

BLUE SHARK

BULL SHARK TOOTH

The bull shark has pointy bottom teeth and triangular top teeth. Its mouth is like a knife and fork. The bottom teeth hold the fish it catches, and the top jaw goes back and forth and cuts like a saw.

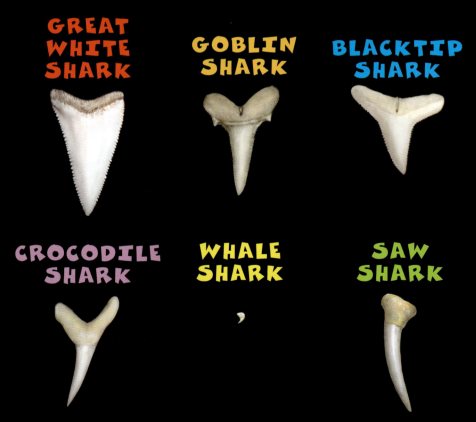

GREAT WHITE SHARK

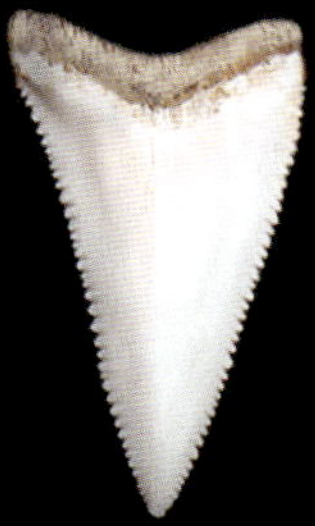

GOBLIN SHARK

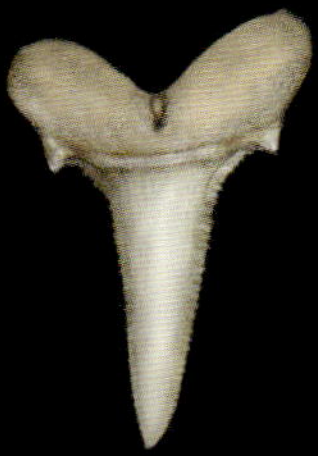

BLACKTIP SHARK

CROCODILE SHARK

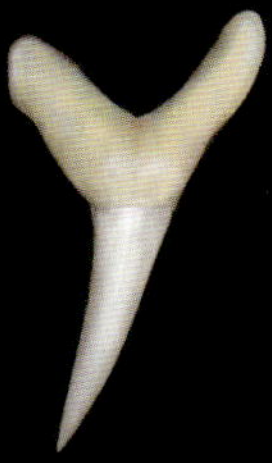

WHALE SHARK

SAW SHARK

ANATOMY OF A HAMMERHEAD

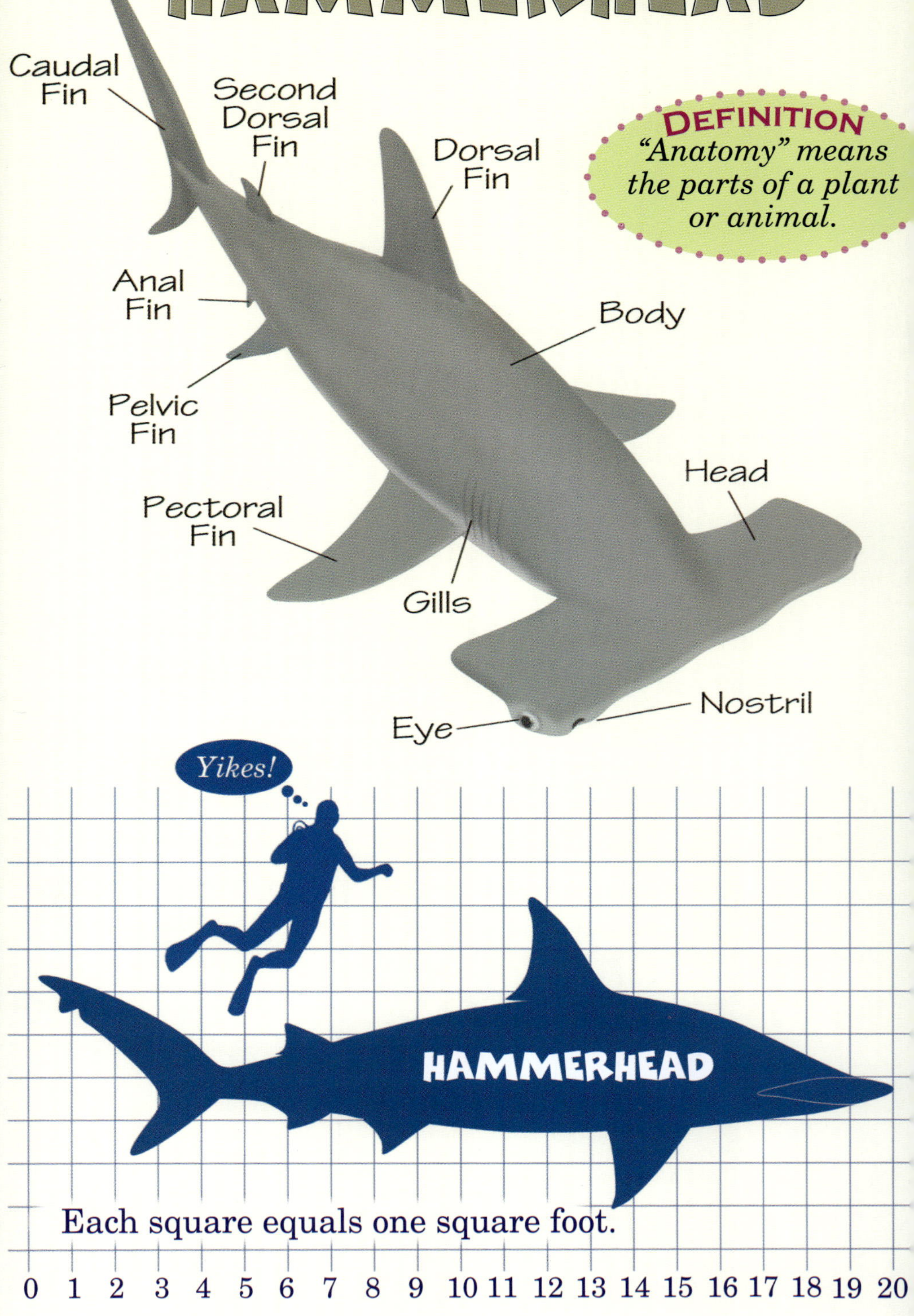

DEFINITION
"Anatomy" means the parts of a plant or animal.

Each square equals one square foot.

ANATOMY OF A BULL SHARK

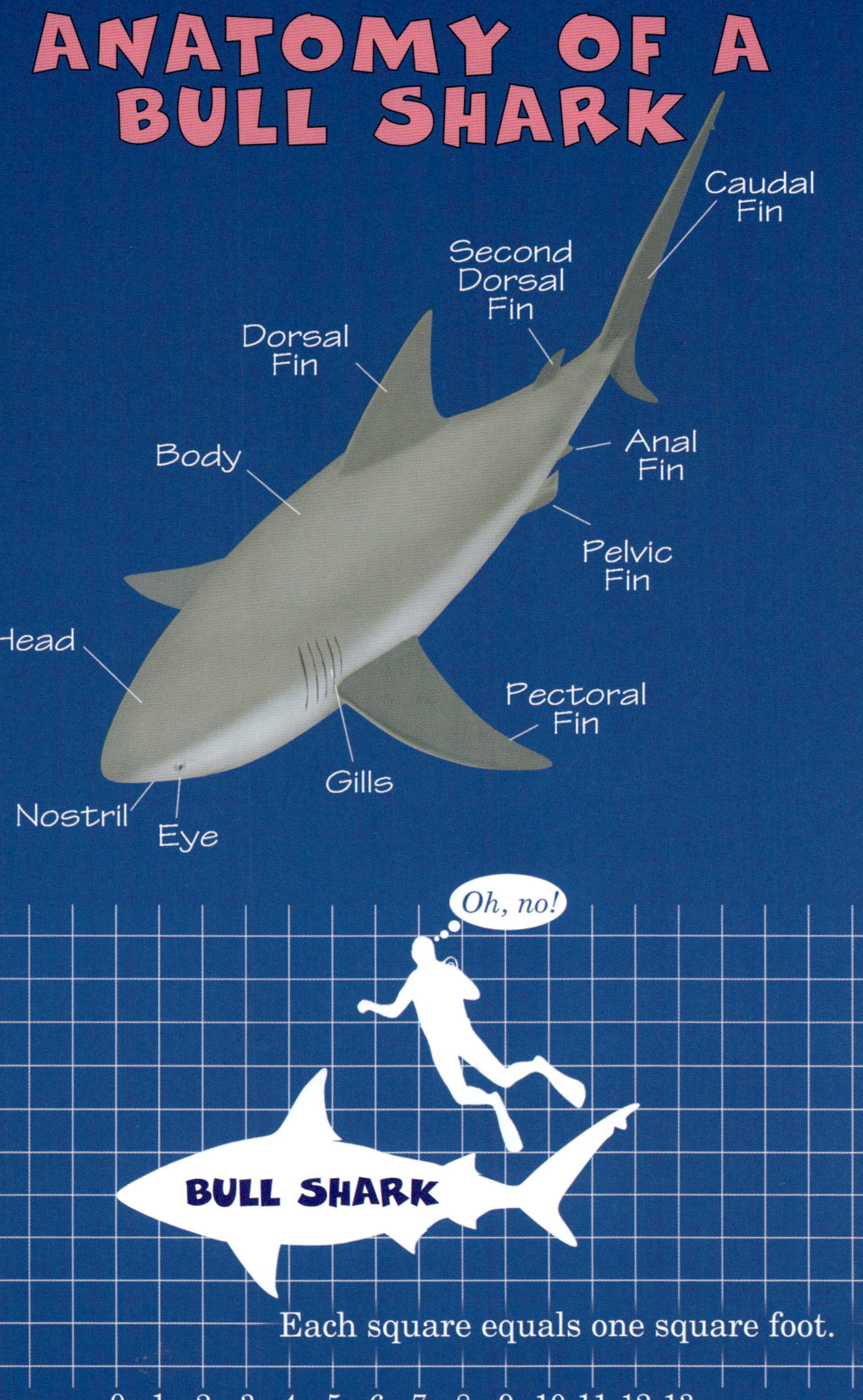

When engineers design aircraft, sometimes all they have to do is look at nature.

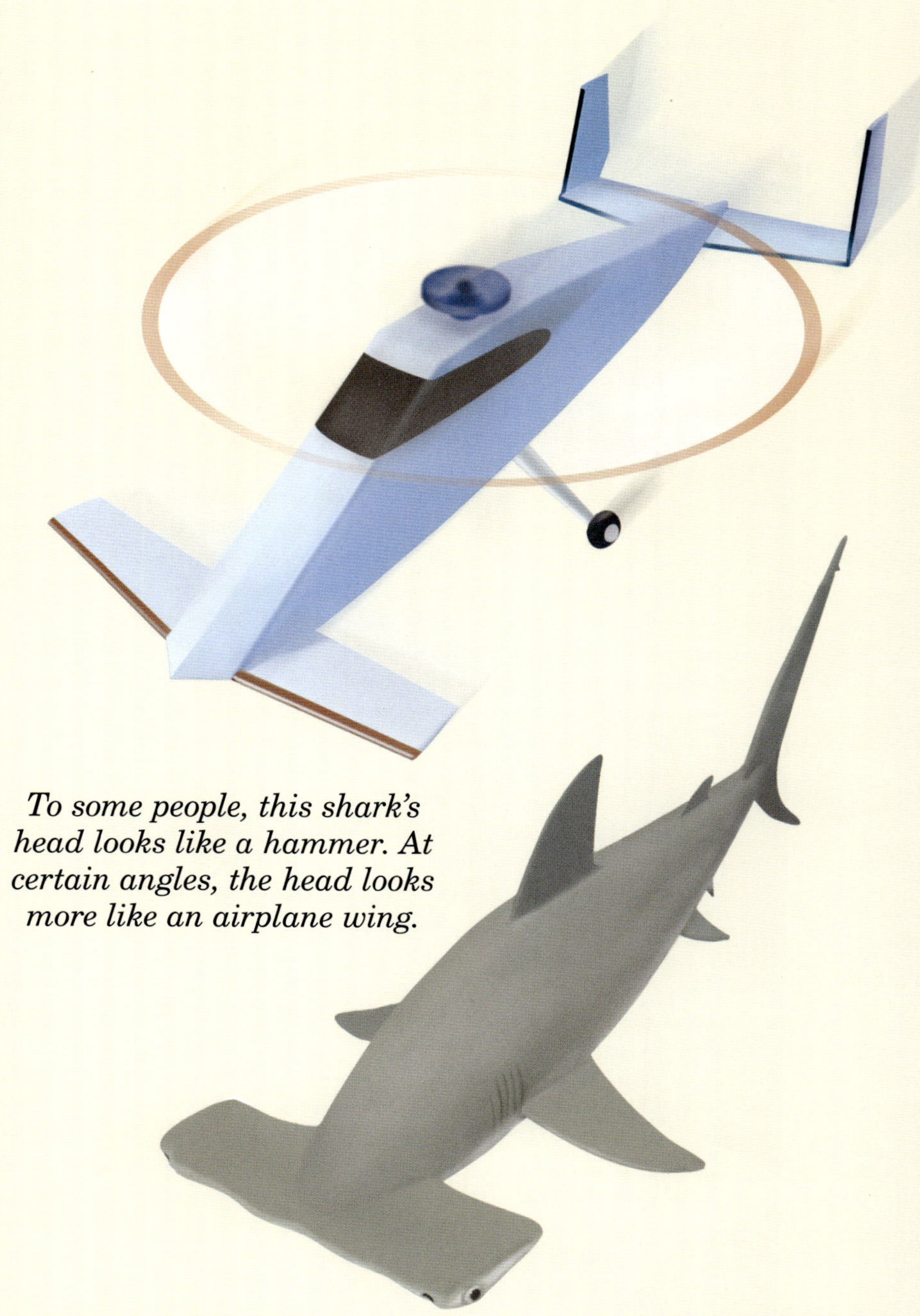

To some people, this shark's head looks like a hammer. At certain angles, the head looks more like an airplane wing.

The wing-shaped head gives the shark stability when it is swimming.

You could say that the space shuttle was designed by nature millions of years ago.

Fun Fact
Aircraft engineers study "aerodynamics."

Look at the shape and design of the bull shark.

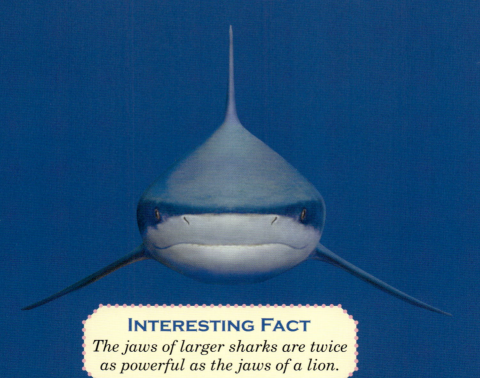

Interesting Fact
The jaws of larger sharks are twice as powerful as the jaws of a lion.

SHARK

The great hammerhead and the bull shark are different sharks, but their tails are similar. Take a look!

GREAT HAMMERHEAD SHARK

FUN FACT

A ragged-tooth shark can touch its tail with its nose

WHALE SHARK

COOKIECUTTER SHARK

NURSE SHARK

BONUS FACT

A tail fin is also called a caudal fin.

TAILS

A shark uses its tail to propel itself forward. It steers with its tail and its side fins.

BULL SHARK

BONUS FACT
Almost all sharks have a vertical tail.

THRESHER SHARK

BLACKTIP REEF SHARK

TIGER SHARK

SHARK FRIENDS

Sharks and pilot fish are friends.

For example, pilot fish eat parasites off the shark's skin. Pilot fish get to eat the shark's leftover food scraps. And pilot fish stay safe from predators by swimming with the shark.

TOUGH FACT

Sharks have rough skin—it is like armor. They have teeth on their skin called denticles.

DID YOU KNOW?

Cleaner wrasses are fish that clean sharks' skin. Some even go in the sharks' mouths.

SHARK HITCHHIKERS

Remoras are fish that hitch a ride on the shark. Remoras have a suction disc and attach themselves.

SHARK TRIVIA

Remoras are also called sharksuckers.

This is a remora.

ICKY FACT

Some parasitic copepods and worms attach themselves to sharks.

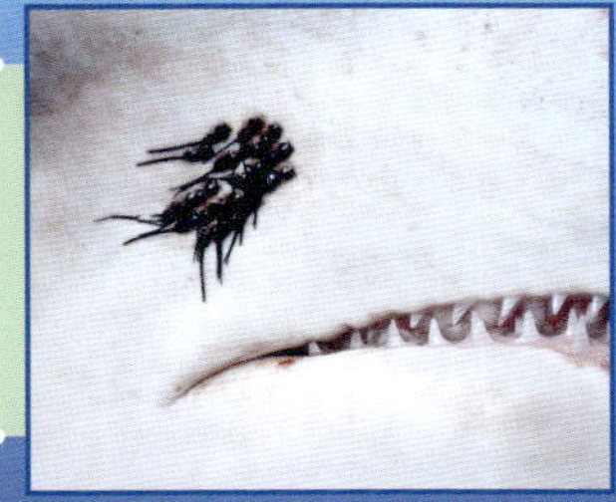

THINGS A HAMMERHEAD SHARK CAN'T DO

They can't parachute.

They can't sing like Elvis.

They can't ride a bicycle.

THINGS A BULL SHARK CAN'T DO

They can't yo-yo.

They can't paint like Michelangelo.

They can't bake cupcakes.

A giant hammerhead is cruising along. A bull shark is looking for food.

Interesting Fact

A hammerhead uses its wide head to detect and pin stingrays to the ocean floor. They are its favorite food.

he hammerhead sees the bull shark, but is not interested. uge sharks are not his type of food. The hammerhead oks for something smaller and easier to eat.

DID YOU KNOW?

The ferocious bull shark easily adapts to captivity and living in an aquarium.

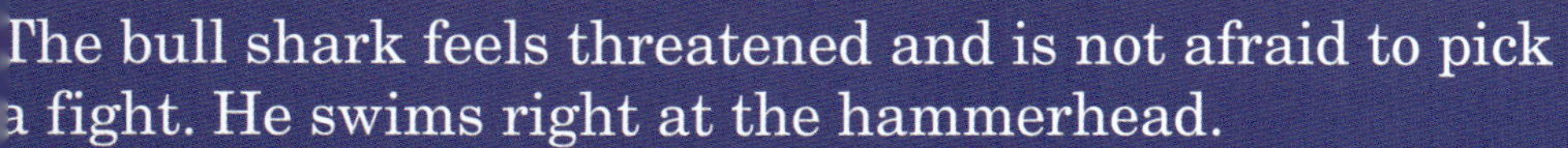

The bull shark feels threatened and is not afraid to pick a fight. He swims right at the hammerhead.

The bull shark opens its mouth and tries to ram the hammerhead. The hammerhead's better eyesight allows him to turn and avoid the bull shark. The hammerhead dodges away.

The bull shark is angry and darts at the hammerhead again. The hammerhead ducks. Both sharks are excellent swimmers.

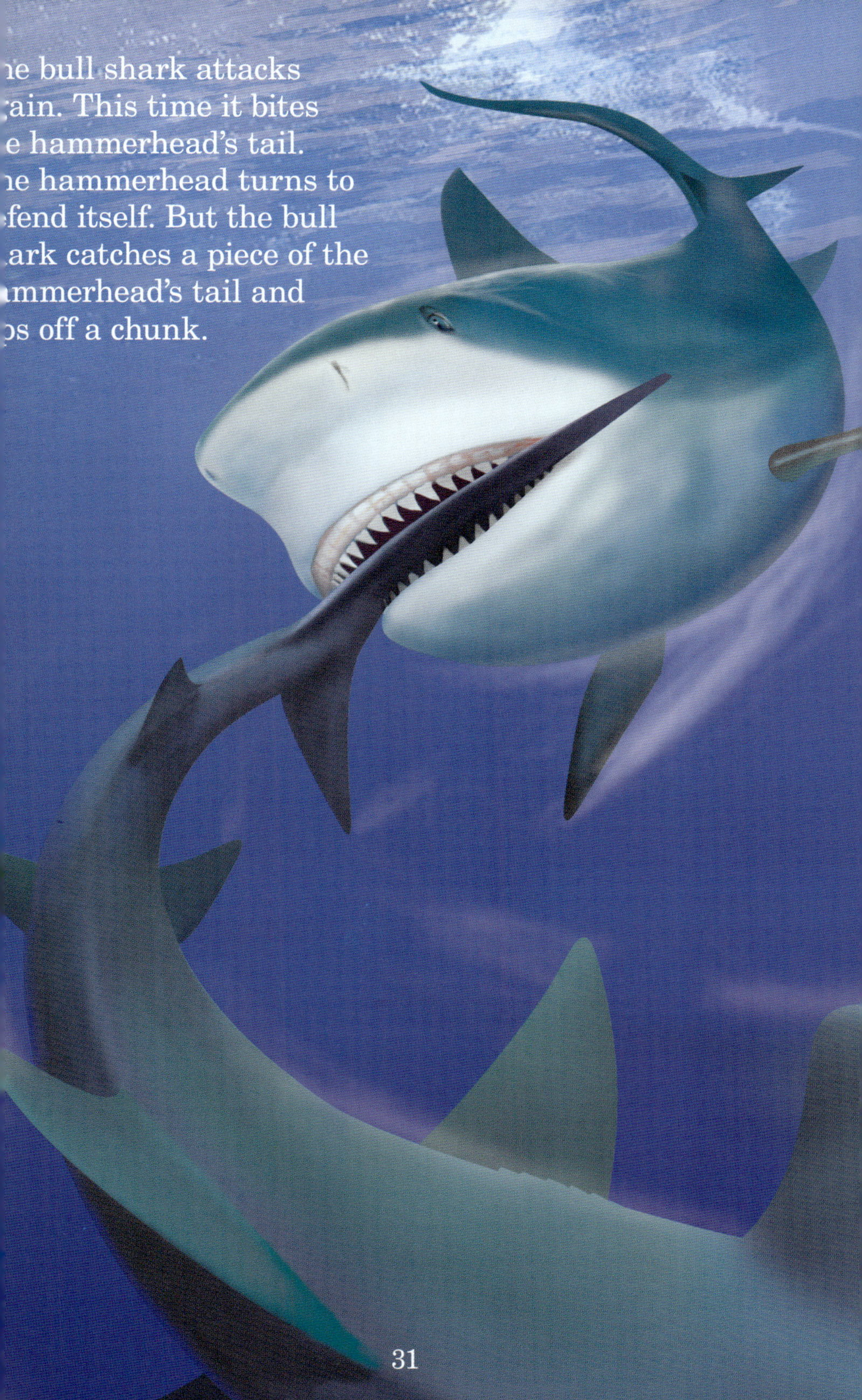

ne bull shark attacks
ain. This time it bites
e hammerhead's tail.
ne hammerhead turns to
fend itself. But the bull
ark catches a piece of the
mmerhead's tail and
os off a chunk.

The hammerhead is bleeding and can't swim as fast. His blood excites the bull shark even more. At full speed the bull shark rams the hammerhead and knocks him off balance. The bull shark bites the hammerhead a few more times.

The hammerhead is defeated. The bull shark will eat him. Other sharks in the area can smell the meal.

The bull shark won today. Maybe the next time these two species meet, the hammerhead will recognize the danger right away.

KILLER WHALE

VS.

GREAT WHITE SHARK

What would happen if a killer whale met up with a great white shark? What if they had a fight? Who do you think would win?

SCIENTIFIC NAME OF KILLER WHALE:

"ORCINUS ORCA"

Meet the killer whale, also known as an orca. It is a sea mammal. It breathes air through the blowhole on the top its head. Just like you, killer whales have lungs. They hol their breath underwater.

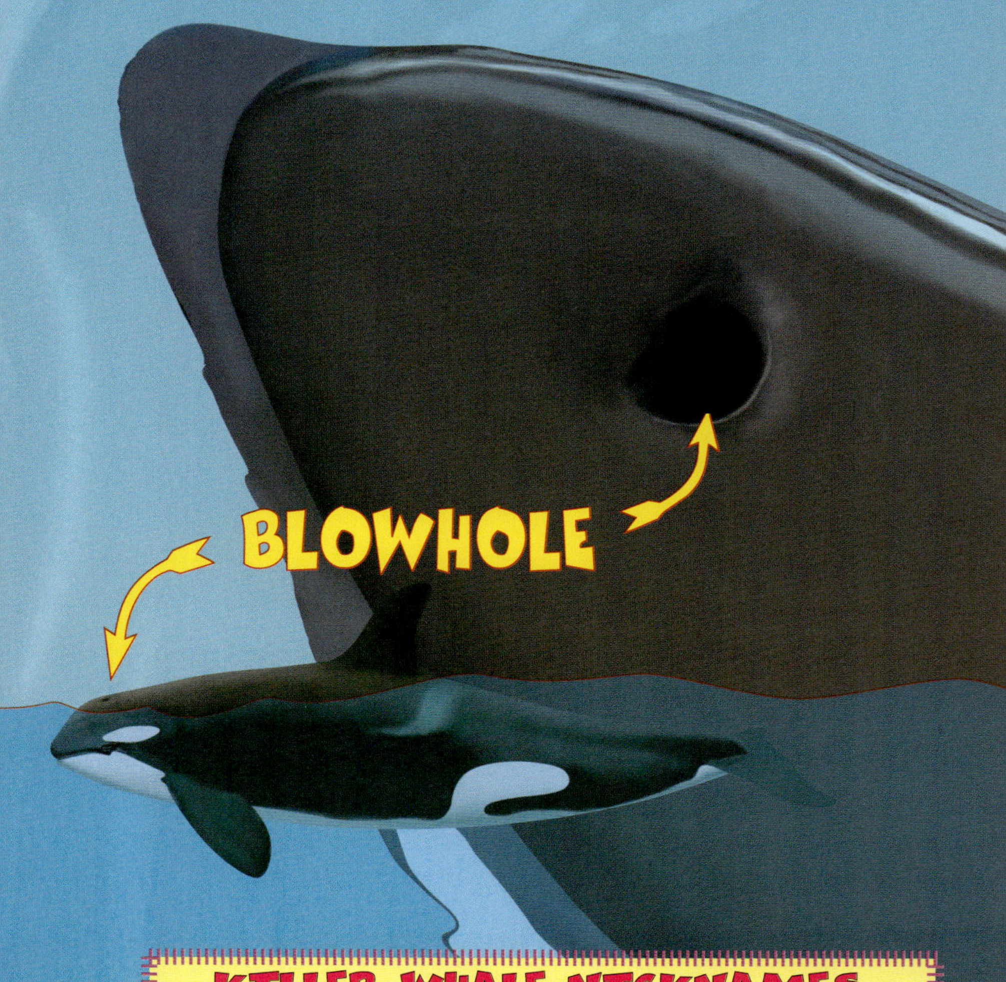

KILLER WHALE NICKNAMES:
BLACKFISH, ORCA, SEAWOLF,
and
KILLER OF WHALES

SCIENTIFIC NAME OF GREAT WHITE SHARK: "CARCHARODON CARCHARIAS"

Ieet the great white shark. It's a huge fish that can't urvive out of the water. Sharks and other fish don't reathe air. Fish get oxygen from water that flows hrough their gills.

Like most sharks, the great white has five gill slits.

GREAT WHITE SHARK NICKNAMES:
MAN-EATER, TOMMY, WHITE POINTER,* and *WHITE DEATH

The killer whale has a huge jaw full of about fifty teeth. The teeth can be almost four inches long.

Gum line
ACTUAL SIZE
A killer whale tooth looks like this!

DID YOU KNOW?

If the killer whale loses an adult tooth, it doesn't grow back.

A great white shark has a gigantic mouth full of several rows of razor-sharp teeth. It's scary just to look at them.

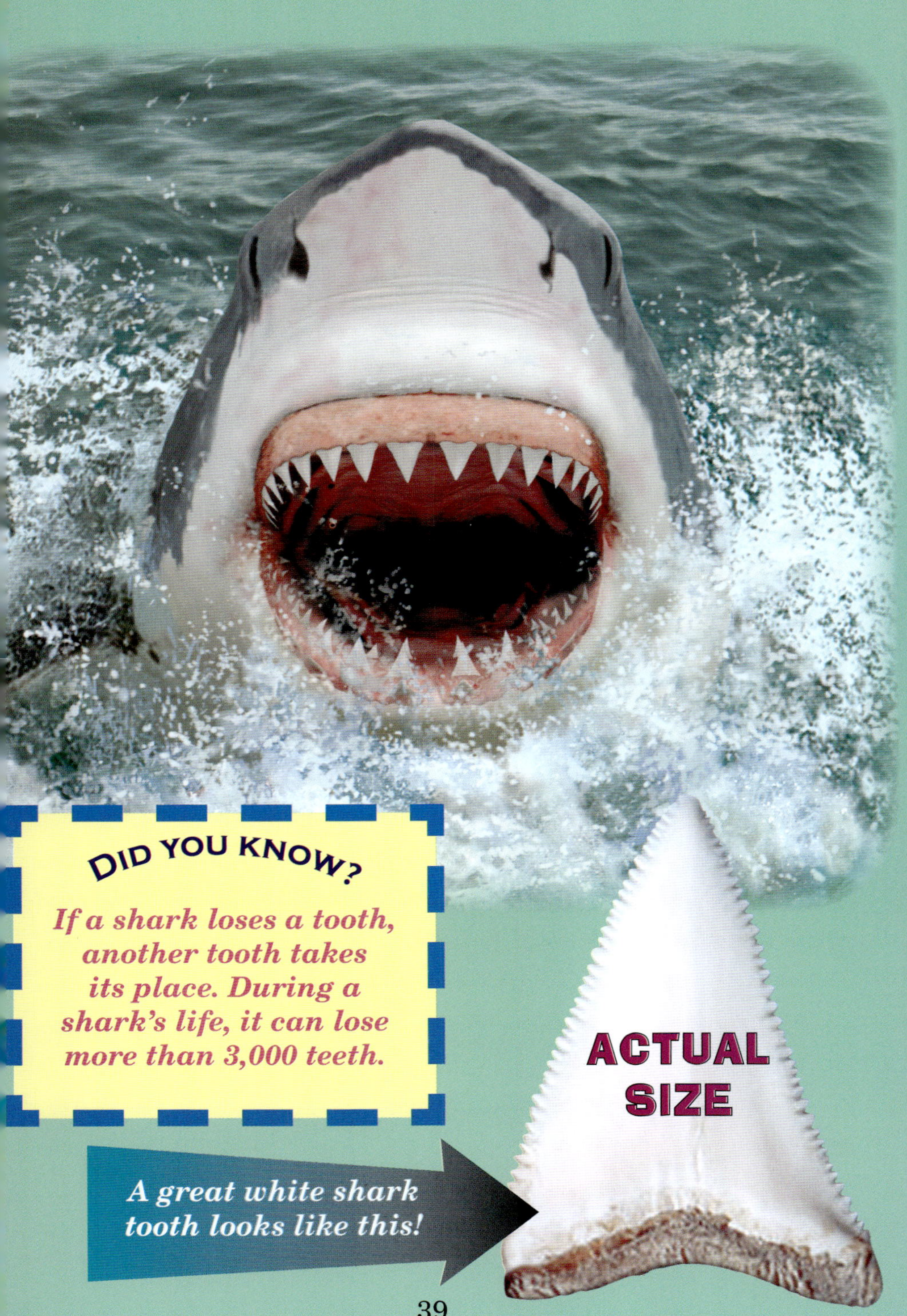

DID YOU KNOW?

If a shark loses a tooth, another tooth takes its place. During a shark's life, it can lose more than 3,000 teeth.

A great white shark tooth looks like this!

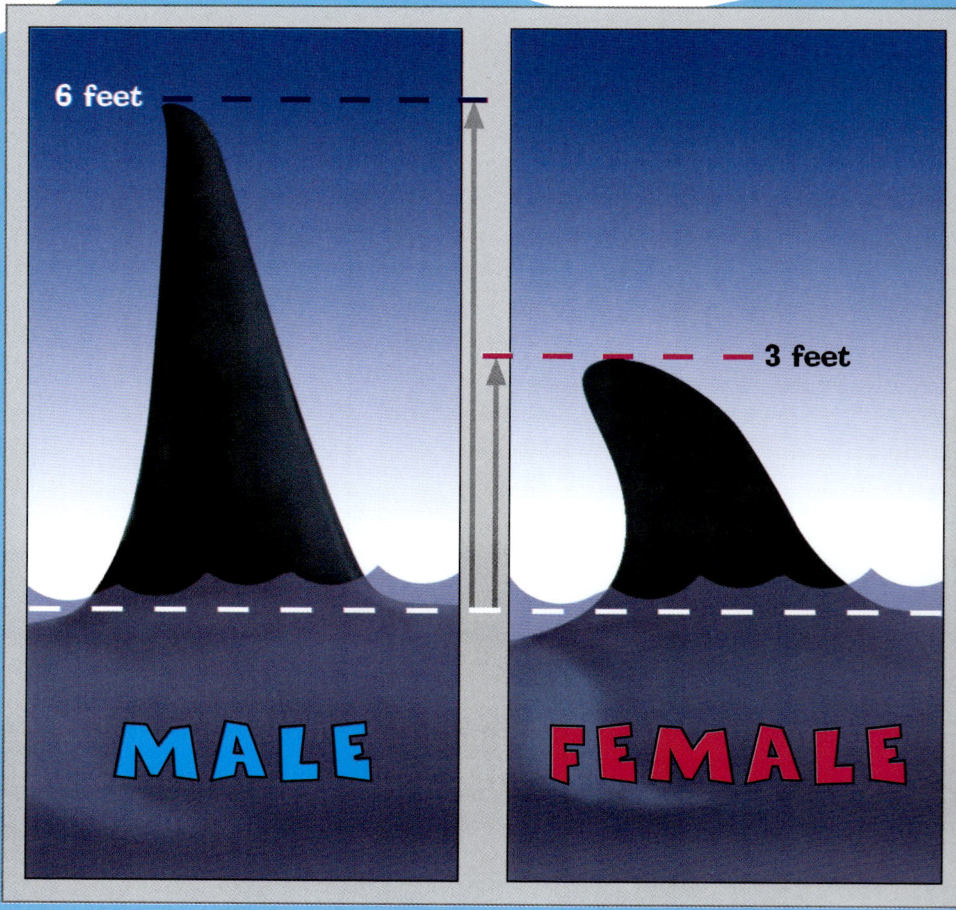

6 feet

3 feet

MALE

FEMALE

The killer whale's dorsal fin looks like these. On a male killer whale, the dorsal fin can be up to six feet tall.

Killer whales can be found in all oceans.

Male and female great white sharks have dorsal fins that look the same.

Great white sharks are also found in all oceans.

Killer whales are meat eaters. Thei favorite foods are seals and sea lions, but they also eat salmon and other fish. A killer whale was once seen grabbing a moose and a deer off the shoreline!

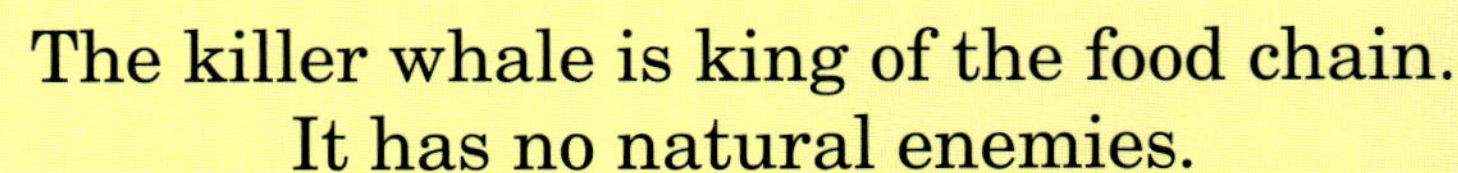

The killer whale is king of the food chain. It has no natural enemies.

The ocean is more like a food web than a food chain. In the ocean, everything eats almost everything else.

Great white sharks eat fish, but have also been known to eat seals, sea lions, and even sea turtles. Now and then, they eat a few people.

A great white shark is also high on the food chain. It is the largest predatory fish.

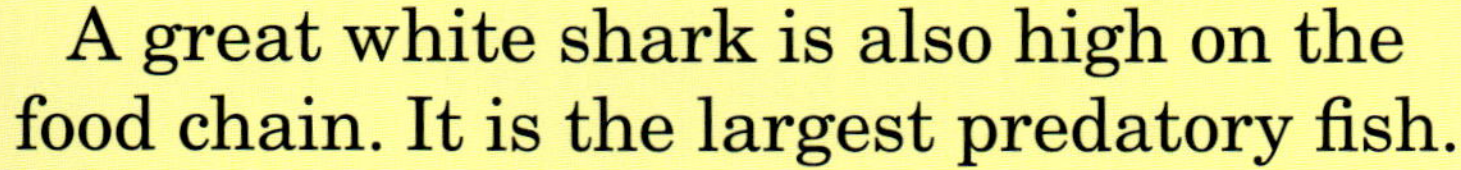

Tiny plankton is eaten by small fish. Small fish get eaten by bigger fish. Bigger fish get eaten by larger fish, and so on.

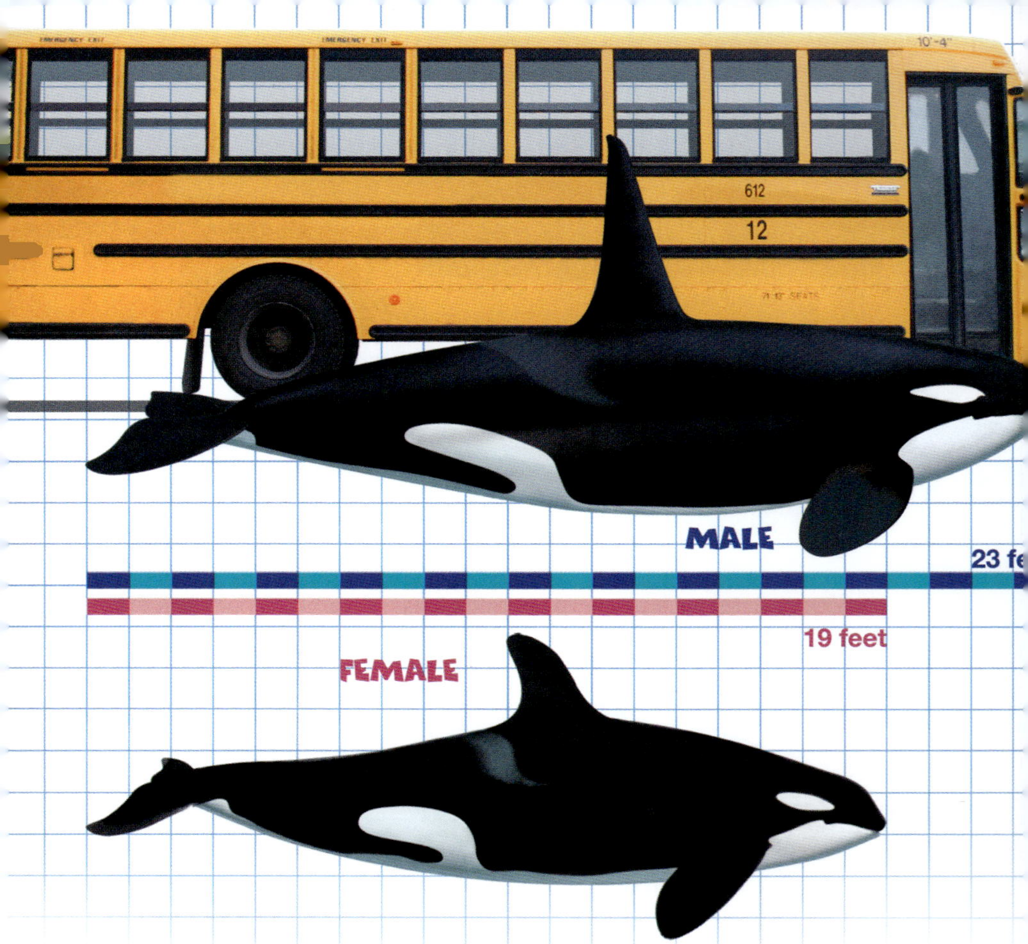

A male killer whale is bigger than a female killer whale
A female is about four feet shorter.

Killer whales have bones. This is a killer whale skeleton.

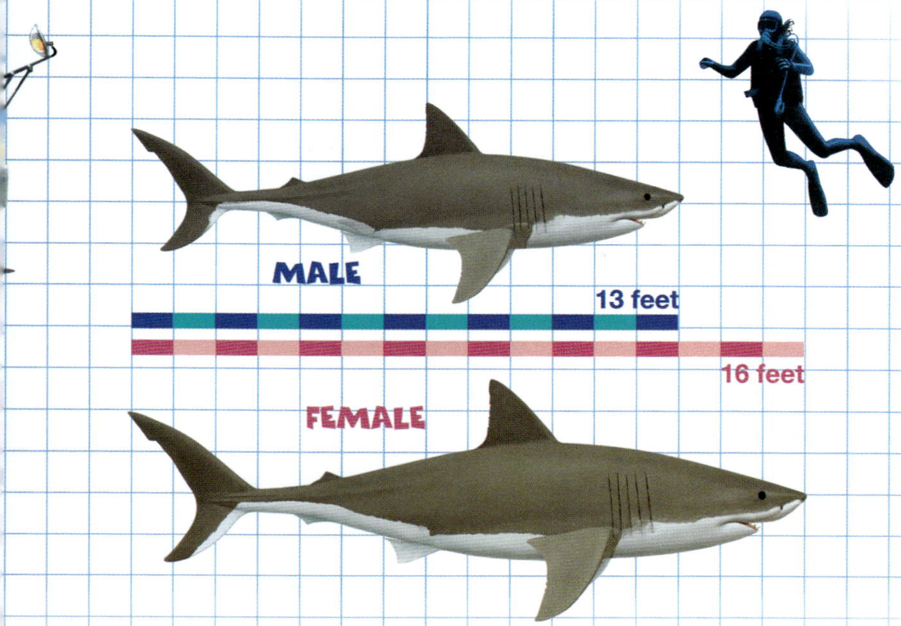

MALE

13 feet

16 feet

FEMALE

The female great white shark is bigger than the male. Females are wider and about three feet longer.

LOOK! NO BONES!

Great white sharks do not have bones. Shark skeletons are made of cartilage. Feel your own ear. It is made of cartilage.

Although they are huge, killer whales can jump completely out of the water.

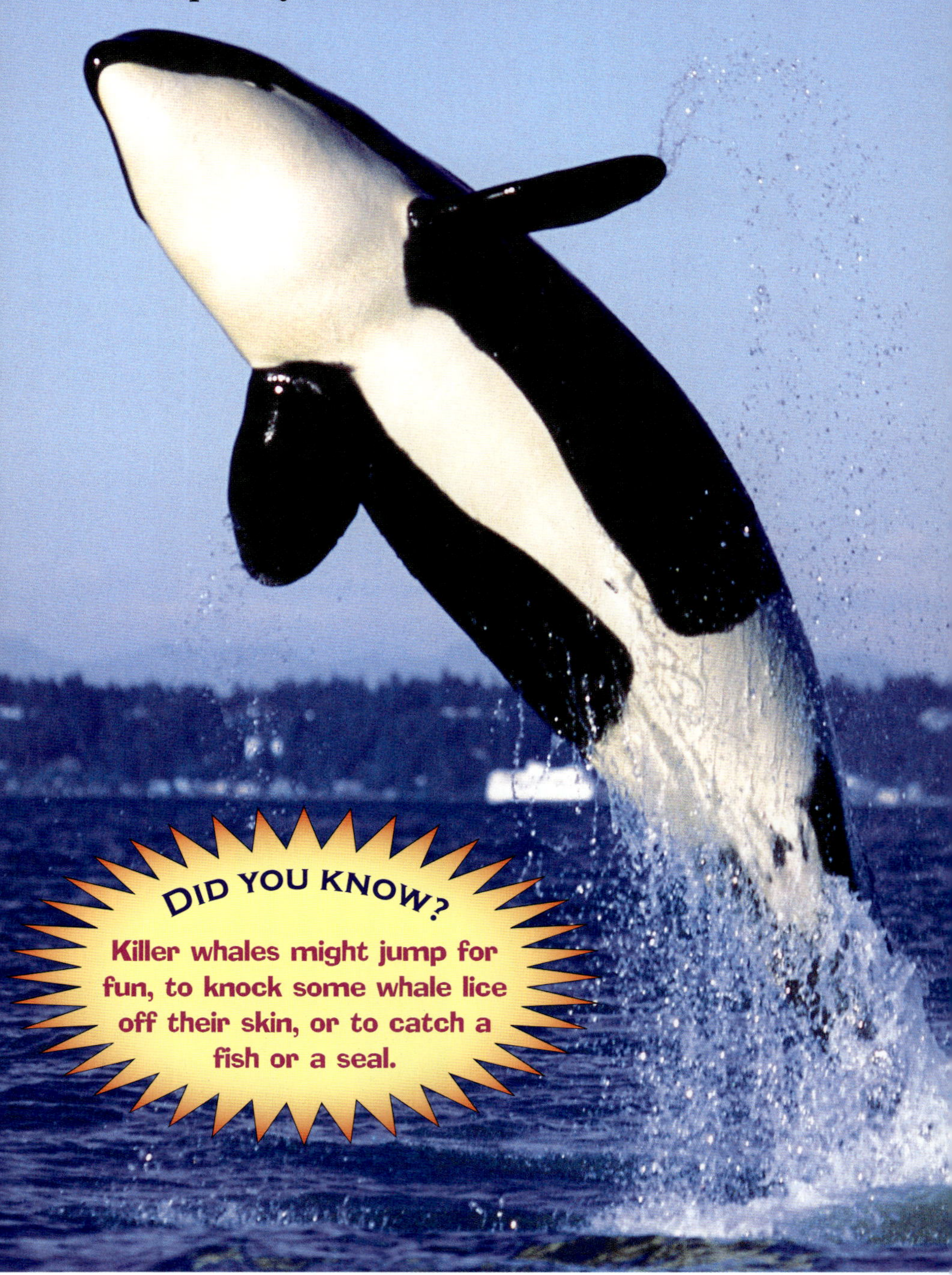

DID YOU KNOW?
Killer whales might jump for fun, to knock some whale lice off their skin, or to catch a fish or a seal.

In a fight, who do you think would win? A killer whale o a great white shark?

DID YOU KNOW?
Great white sharks have been seen leaping into the air to catch a seal or a sea lion.

Wow! Great white sharks can jump completely out of the water too!

So look at the facts! Who do you think has an advantage? Who would win?

Like other sea mammals, killer whales have a horizontal tail.

DID YOU KNOW?

Killer whales can swim with just their side fins, but their huge tail is used for speed and turning. A horizontal tail is a better design for diving and surfacing fast.

Like other sharks, a great white shark has a vertical tail.

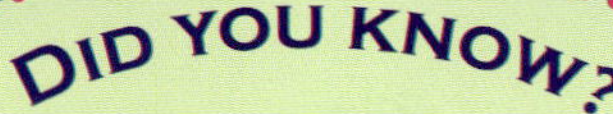

Great white sharks and other fish use their tails for speed and steering.

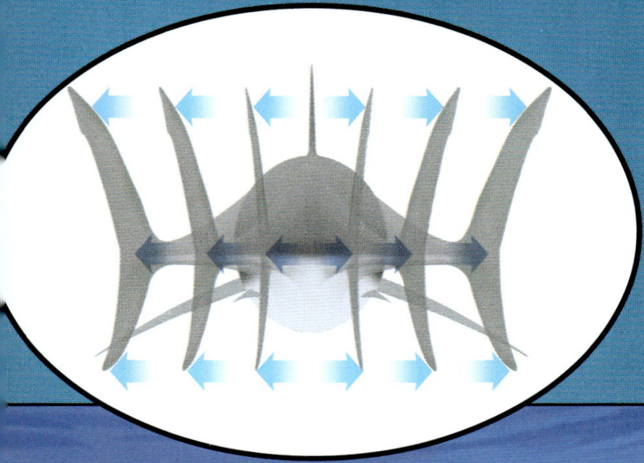

SONAR

Killer whales have no ears. They bounce sounds off of approaching fish. They use sonar to navigate, to locate other creatures in the ocean, and to find each other. They recognize echoes and other vibrations in the water. This is called echolocation.

Bonus Fact!

SONAR

is an acronym:

SOund
Navigation
And
Ranging

DID YOU KNOW?

Submarines also us sonar, but nature had it first. Bats use sonar too

Underwater, you look like thi a killer whal

SMELL

DID YOU KNOW?
Sharks can smell blood from three miles away!

Underwater, the great white shark senses your electricity.

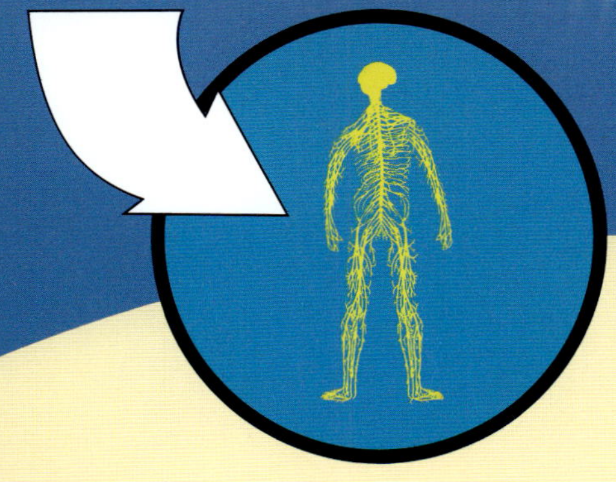

Great white sharks have a keen sense of smell. They can also detect the electricity in fish and other animals. They can tell if you are nervous.

Killer whales are family oriented. They live in groups called pods. Killer whale moms, dads, aunts, uncles, cousins, and kids eat, swim, and play together. They look out for each other.

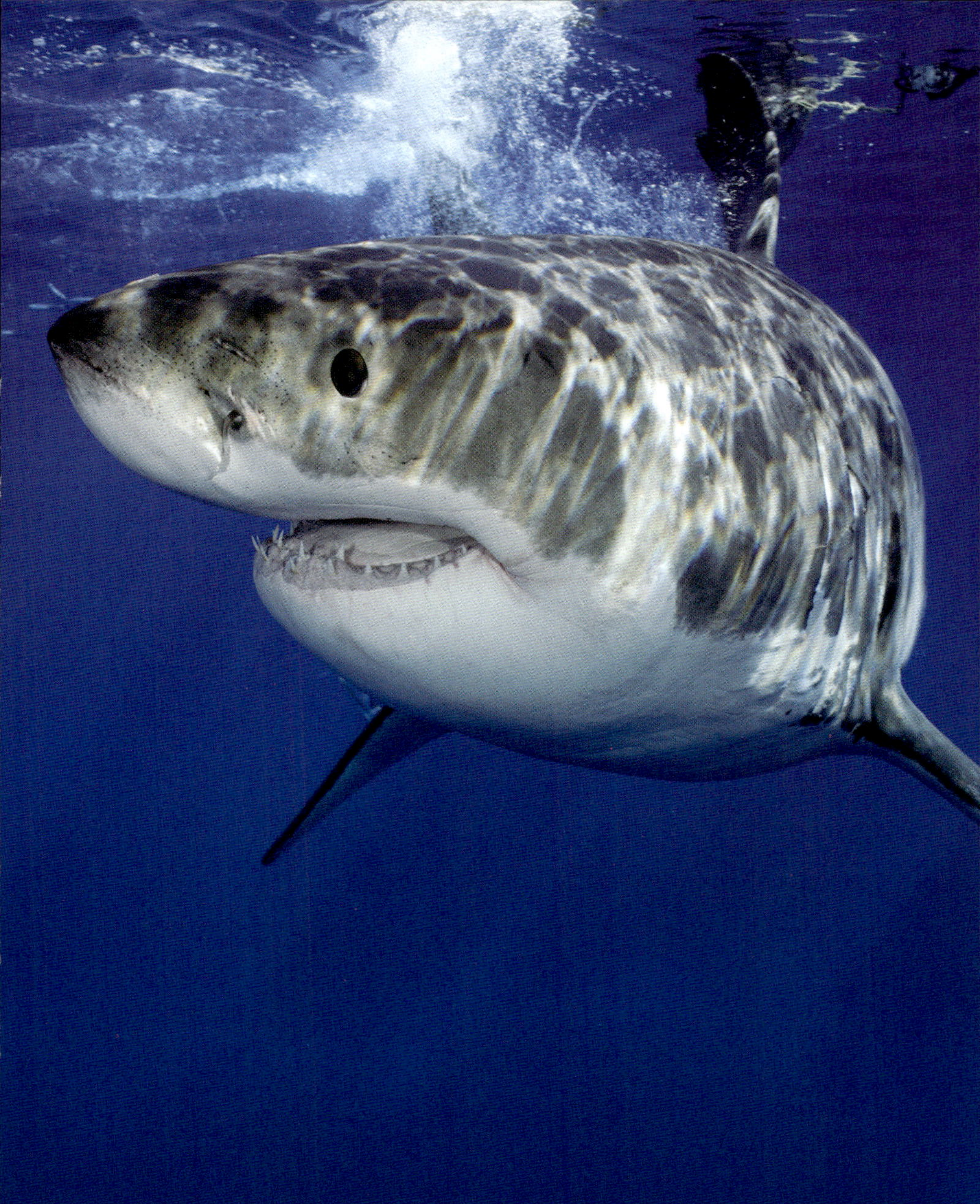

Great white sharks are loners. Two and three have been seen hunting as a team. But mostly they travel, hunt, and eat alone.

Killer whales can stop swimming and tread water in one place. They can swim up to thirty miles per hour. In the ocean, that is fast!

DID YOU KNOW?
Killer whales have smooth skin.

Great white sharks never stop swimming. Seawater must flow through their gills so they can get oxygen. They cruise along at about two miles per hour, but speed up in bursts to twenty miles per hour.

Great white sharks have rough skin. It is like sandpaper. Most fish have scales. Sharks have denticles. Denticles are like little tiny teeth on their skin.

CLOSE-UP OF THE DENTICLES ON A GREAT WHITE'S SKIN

Killer Whale Brain

A killer whale's brain looks similar to a human brain, but is three times larger. Killer whales are extremely intelligent.

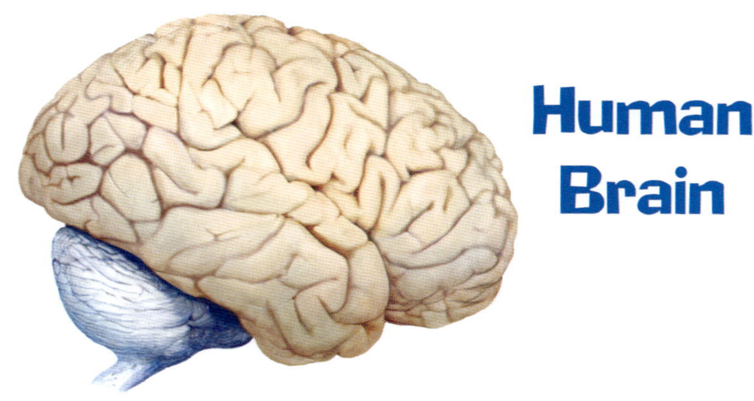

Great White Shark Brain

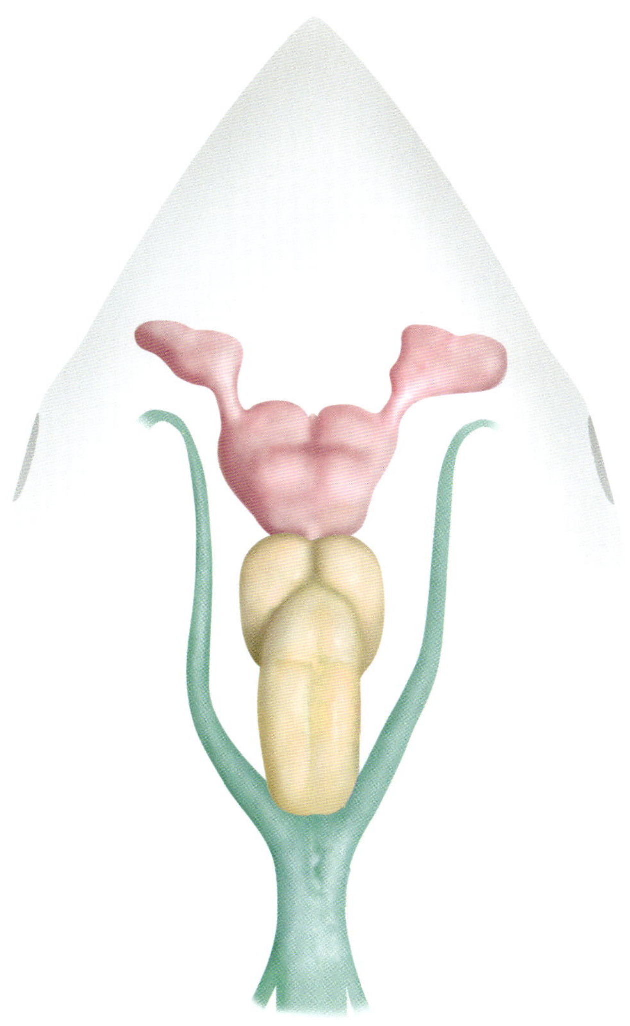

A great white shark does not have a round brain. It has different sections connected together. It is shaped like a letter "Y." Scientists think every section is connected to a different sense.

A killer whale can be captured, live in captivity, and trained to perform tricks. Killer whales were once stars at aquariums and amusement parks.

reat white sharks have never been able to survive long
captivity. Hollywood loves to make movies about them.
reat white sharks are movie stars!

WHO WOULD WIN?
now playing
KILLER WHALE
VS.
GREAT WHITE SHARK
FUN FACT:
Jaws is one of the most popular movies of all time. For years, moviegoers were afraid to swim at the beach. Everyone knows the music: Dun! Dun! Dun! Dun! Dun! Dun!

So, what would happen if a killer whale and a great white shark met in the ocean?

What if they were the same size?
What if they were both hungry?
What if they had a fight?

Uh-oh! They are in the same place at the same time! They sense each other. There is intense competition in nature. They are each planning their attacks!

Great white sharks like to attack from below. Killer whales like to attack from any side. They are getting closer. Then the fight happens.

The great white shark makes the first move. It tries to attack with its sharp teeth. The killer whale outsmarts the shark and bites it. One! Two! Three seconds! The fight is over! It is no contest! The ferocious great white shark doesn't know what hit it.

The killer whale won today. What do you think will happen the next time a killer whale meets a great white shark? Who would win? Do you think the shark can overcome a killer whale's superior intelligence?

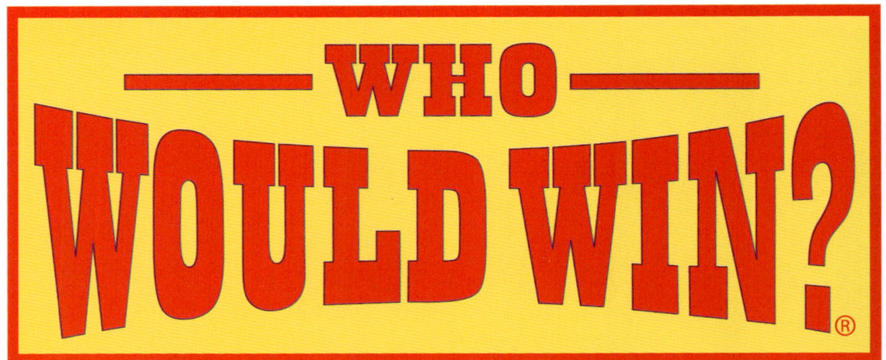

LOBSTER

VS.

CRAB

What if a lobster and a crab bumped into each other. What if they had a fight? Who do you think would win?

WHICH LOBSTER?

Which lobster should fight the crab?

SPINY LOBSTER

Spiny lobster from the Caribbean? Sorry, you are spiky, but have no claws.

PINK SPOTTED PRAWN

Pink spotted prawn? No way! You are a shrimp, not a lobster.

Shovel-nosed lobster? Nope, you are strange looking. Go dig up a clam!

SHOVEL-NOSED LOBSTER

American lobster? Perfect! Two claws.

AMERICAN LOBSTER

WHICH CRAB?

Which crab should fight the lobster?

DUNGENESS CRAB

Dungeness crab? No! It is famous in San Francisco and on the West Coast. Its shell is rubbery.

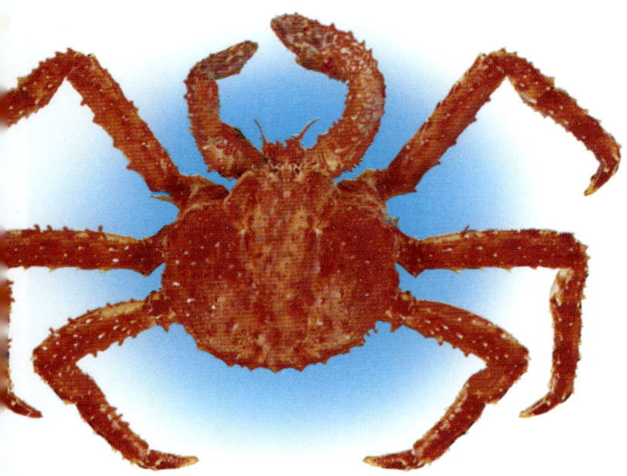

ALASKAN KING CRAB

Alaskan king crab? No! You have only six legs. You are popular in restaurants all over the world.

FACT
Crabs have eight legs and two claws.

HORSESHOE CRAB

Horseshoe crab? No! You are not even a crab. You look prehistoric!

BLUE CRAB

Blue crab? Yes, you are one of the best-known crabs in the world. And maybe the best tasting.

MEET THE LOBSTER

The American lobster's scientific name is *Homarus americanus*. It lives off America's northeast and Canada's east coasts.

FACT
Lobsters have a muscular tail.

FACT
Lobsters are in an animal family called crustaceans.

WILD FACT
A lobster's teeth are in its stomach.

The largest lobster was about three feet long and weighed 44 pounds.

MEET THE BLUE CRAB

This is a blue crab. It is the most popular crab in the world. Its scientific name is *Callinectes sapidus,* which means "beautiful savory swimmer."

DEFINITION
Savory means pleasant or agreeable in taste or smell.

BITE FACT
A blue crab can't bite with its mouth. A grinding mill inside its body chews its food.

DID YOU KNOW?
Blue crabs are known as "swimming crabs."

DID YOU KNOW?
A blue crab does not have a tail.

The largest blue crab was about one foot wide and weighed a little more than one pound.

WHERE DO LOBSTERS LIVE

American lobsters live from North Carolina's coastline up to Canada's east coast. Lobsters can be found in shallow water close to shore and also in deep water miles out.

WHERE DO CRABS LIVE?

Blue crabs are most often found from the south shore of Cape Cod in Massachusetts all the way down to the Texas-Mexico border. Chesapeake Bay is one of the most famous places for blue crabs.

FACT
Chesapeake Bay is an estuary. An estuary is where the ocean meets a river.

U.S.A.

Range of the blue crab in the U.S.

BONUS FACT
More than 150 rivers and streams empty into the Chesapeake Bay.

DID YOU KNOW?
Blue crabs love shallow, brackish water.

DEFINITION
Brackish water is part salt and part freshwater.

LOBSTER PARTS

The lobster's head and thorax is one piece. It's called a *cephalothorax*. A lobster has eight legs, just like a spider and a scorpion.

On land, lobsters cannot walk well. The front two legs on each side have pincers on them.

CRAB ANATOMY

The blue crab's body is one piece. Its shell is called a *carapace*.

RUNNING FACT
A blue crab walks and runs sideways.

WALKING FACT
A soldier crab is one of the few crabs that walks forward.

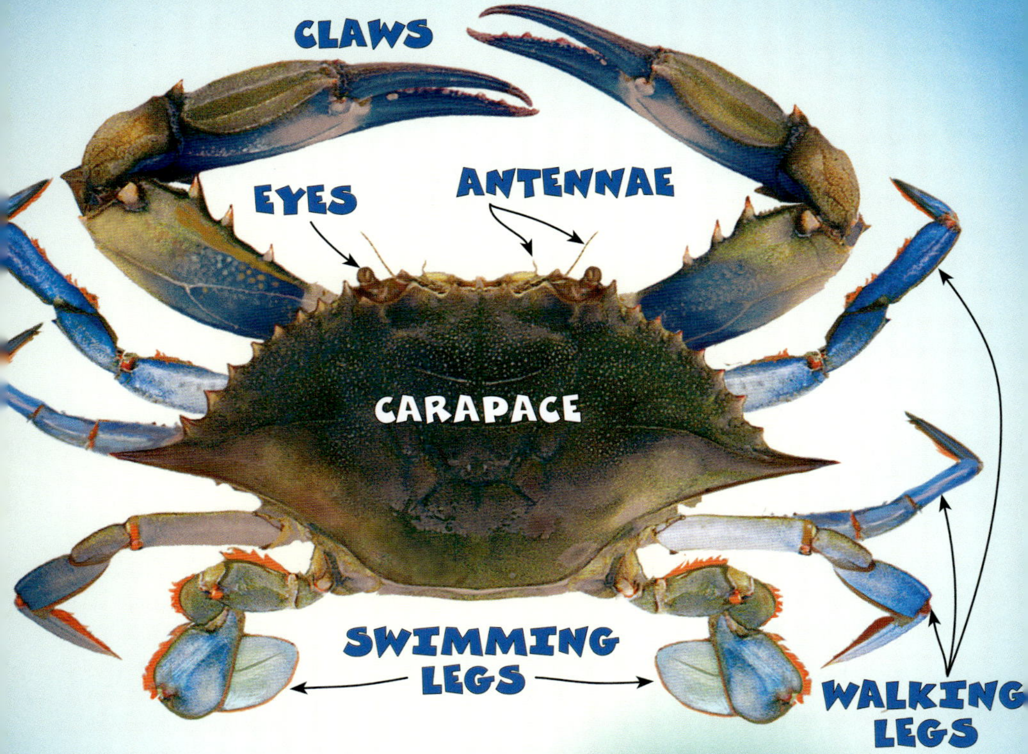

CLAWS

EYES

ANTENNAE

CARAPACE

SWIMMING LEGS

WALKING LEGS

SWIMMING FACT
The last pair of legs on a blue crab are shaped like fins.

Blue crabs can swim well, and they're also great runners. They can run fast on land.

BOY

The crusher claw of a male lobster is bigger and wider than a female crusher claw. The flaps under the tail are called swimmerettes.

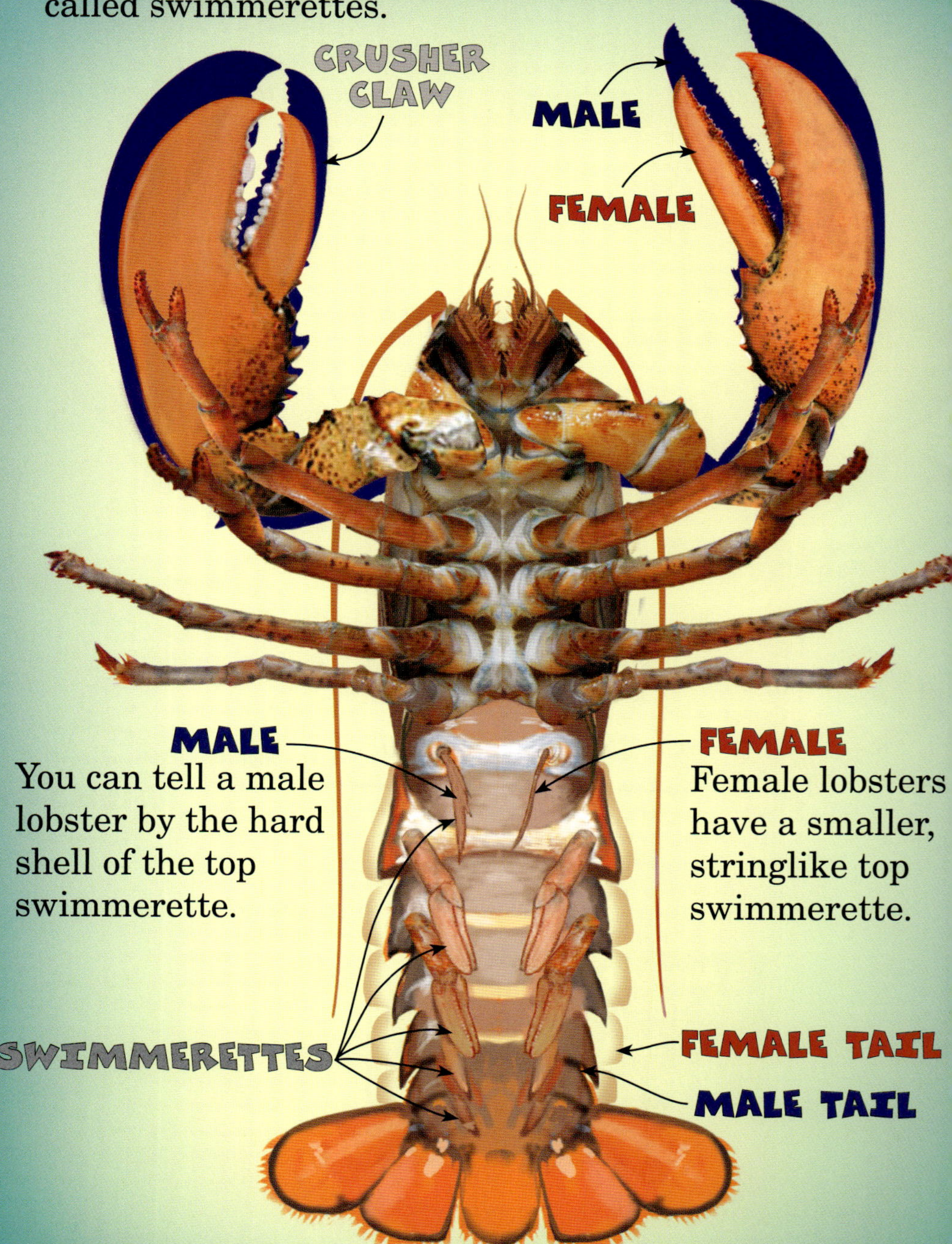
CRUSHER CLAW
MALE
FEMALE
MALE
You can tell a male lobster by the hard shell of the top swimmerette.
FEMALE
Female lobsters have a smaller, stringlike top swimmerette.
SWIMMERETTES
FEMALE TAIL
MALE TAIL

Female lobster tails are wider than male lobster tails.

OR GIRL!

rabs have a flap between their eight legs that is called n apron or a leaf. The girls' leaf is shaped like the apitol Dome. Girl blue crabs also have red tips on their laws. They look like painted fingernails.

CAPITOL DOME

FEMALE LEAF

TERM
A "she-crab" is a young female crab.

3oy blue crabs have a skinny leaf. Some say it is shaped ike the Washington Monument.

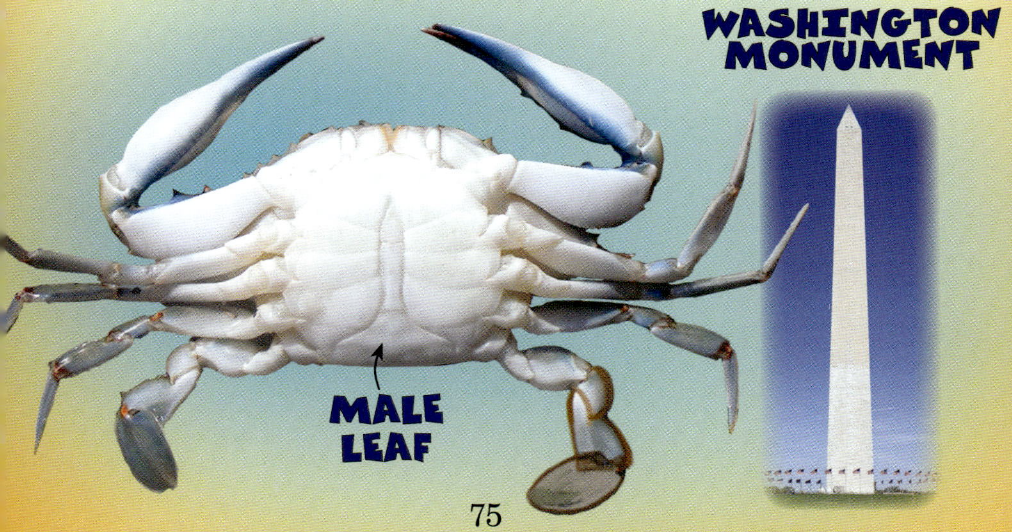

LOBSTER CLAWS

The two claws of a lobster are different. The crusher claw is dull and the scissor claw is sharp.

The crusher claw is slower and strong and usually wider. The scissor claw is quicker and skinnier.

DID YOU KNOW?
Some kids call them a cruncher claw and a ripper claw. Other kids call them a smasher claw and a slasher claw.

Either claw could be on the right or the left.

CRAB PINCERS

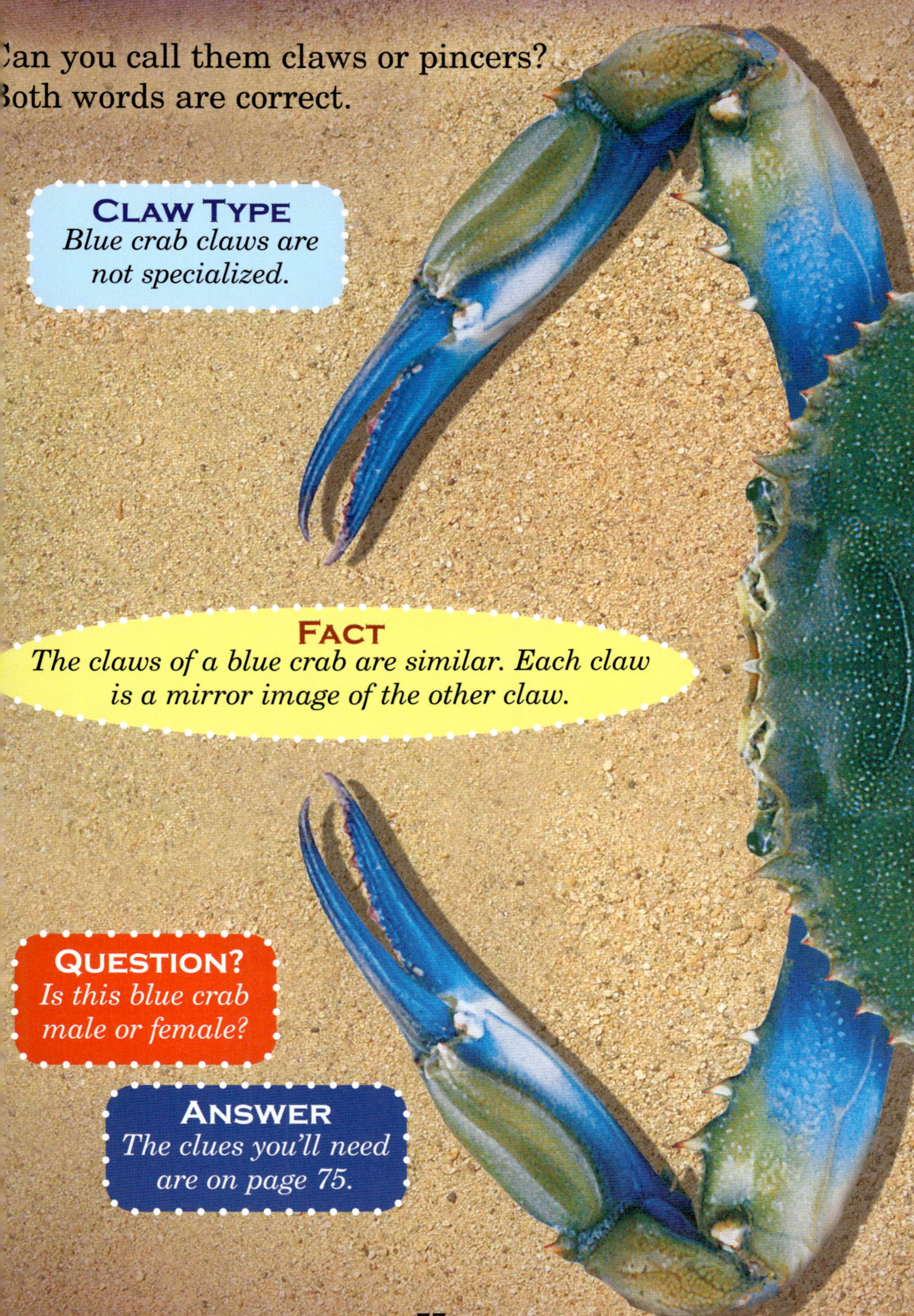

Can you call them claws or pincers? Both words are correct.

CLAW TYPE
Blue crab claws are not specialized.

FACT
The claws of a blue crab are similar. Each claw is a mirror image of the other claw.

QUESTION?
Is this blue crab male or female?

ANSWER
The clues you'll need are on page 75.

LOBSTER BAIT

Most lobsters are caught by traps. Traps are baited with fish heads, fish guts, and fish bones.

SYNONYM
Lobster traps are also called lobster pots.

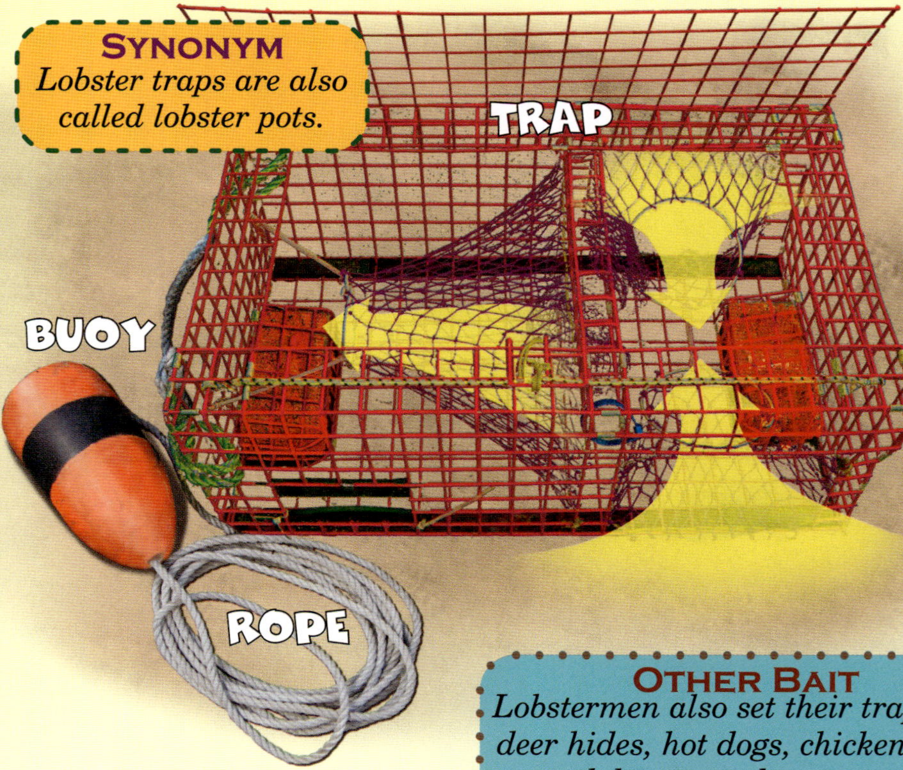

TRAP

BUOY

ROPE

OTHER BAIT
Lobstermen also set their traps wi deer hides, hot dogs, chicken neck steak bones, and even roadkill!

BUOY COLOR?

A buoy is a marker that floats on top of the water. Lobstermen can tell their gear by the colors of the buoy.

QUESTION?
If you were a lobsterman lobsterwoman, what colo would your buoy be?

CATCH A CRAB

Blue crabs are caught by crab pots, trotlines, and by a dip net.

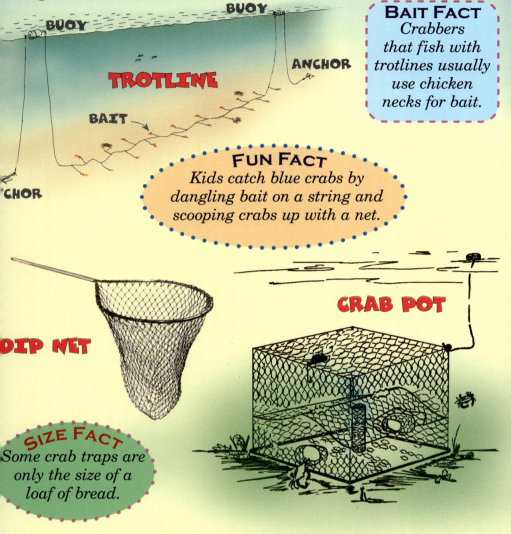

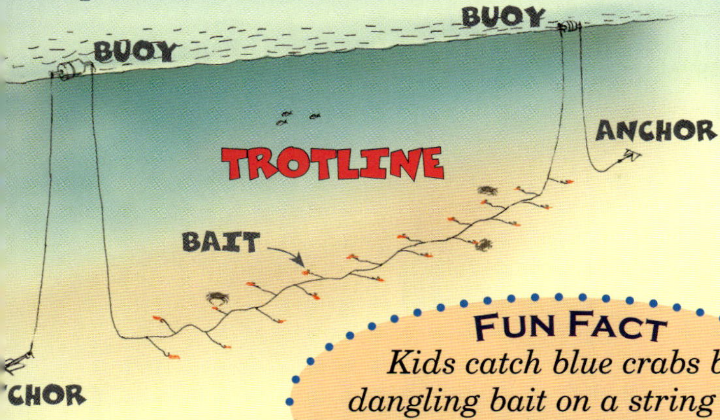

BUOY
BUOY
TROTLINE
ANCHOR
BAIT
CHOR

BAIT FACT
Crabbers that fish with trotlines usually use chicken necks for bait.

FUN FACT
Kids catch blue crabs by dangling bait on a string and scooping crabs up with a net.

DIP NET

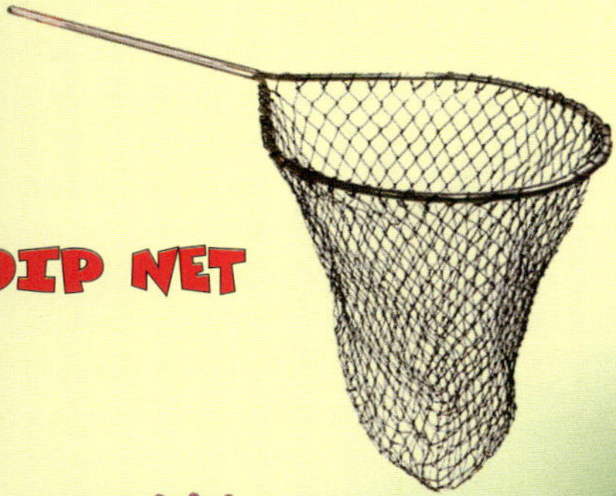

CRAB POT

SIZE FACT
Some crab traps are only the size of a loaf of bread.

Crabs love fresh bait. Chicken, fish, steak, or any meat works well.

EXOSKELETON

Lobsters have an exoskeleton, which is a hard shell on the outside of their bodies. To grow larger, lobsters have to clim out of their shells and then grow a larger shell. This is calle molting.

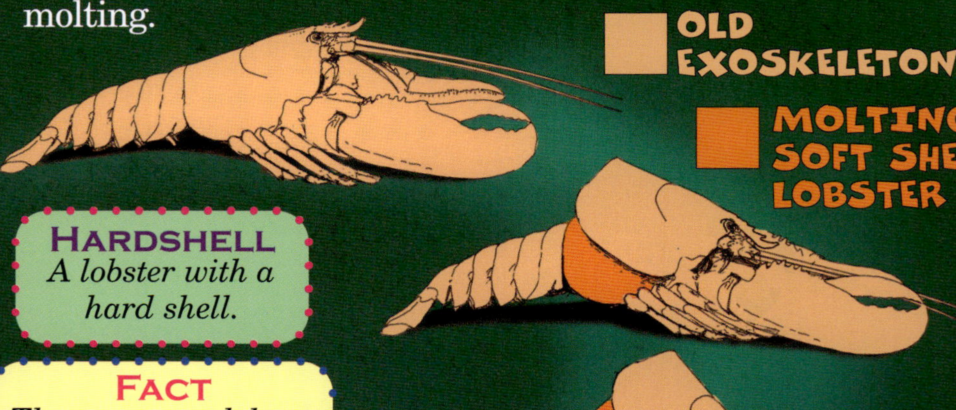

HARDSHELL
A lobster with a hard shell.

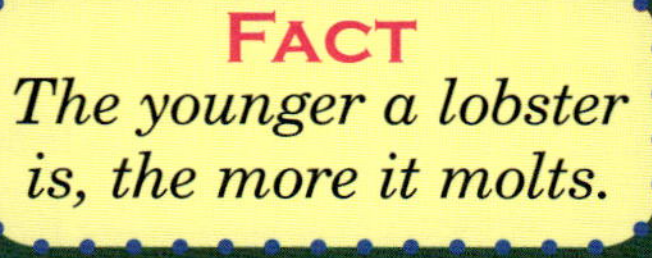

FACT
The younger a lobster is, the more it molts.

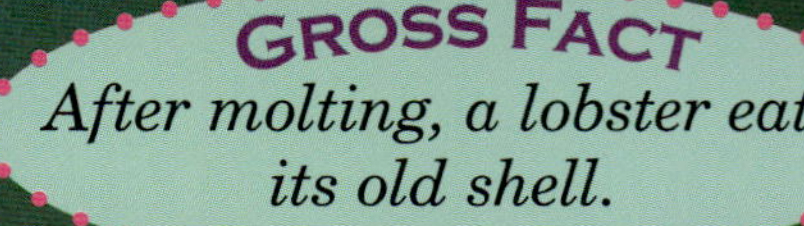

GROSS FACT
After molting, a lobster eats its old shell.

SOFT SHELL
A recently molted lobster whose shell is delicate.

MOLTING

Crabs also have an exoskeleton and molt to grow larger.

DID YOU KNOW?
A "peeler" is a crab about to shed its shell.

DEFINITION
A "hardshell" is a crab that is not molting and has a hard shell.

SOFT FACT
A "soft shell" is a crab that has just shed its shell.

FACT
crustacean that molts is nerable to predators while in a soft state.

EGGER

A female lobster with eggs is called an egger or a seede
She carries the eggs, which are dark green, under her t
attached to her body and swimmerettes.

DID YOU KNOW?
Out of 50,000 eggs, it is estimated that only two grow up to be as large as their mother.

The eggs turn light orange and hatch. The mom lobster carries between 3,000 and 75,000 eggs.

TASTY FACT
One day after hatching, about half the eggs get eaten by fish and other predators.

BABY LOBSTER

SPONGER

ponger is a female crab with eggs. The crab below is a nale blue crab whose leaf is full of eggs.

Scientists think there are up to two million eggs in a large blue crab.

BABY BLUE CRAB

LOBSTER EYES

Lobsters can't see well. They have antennae that sense vibrations in the water. They have a great sense of smel

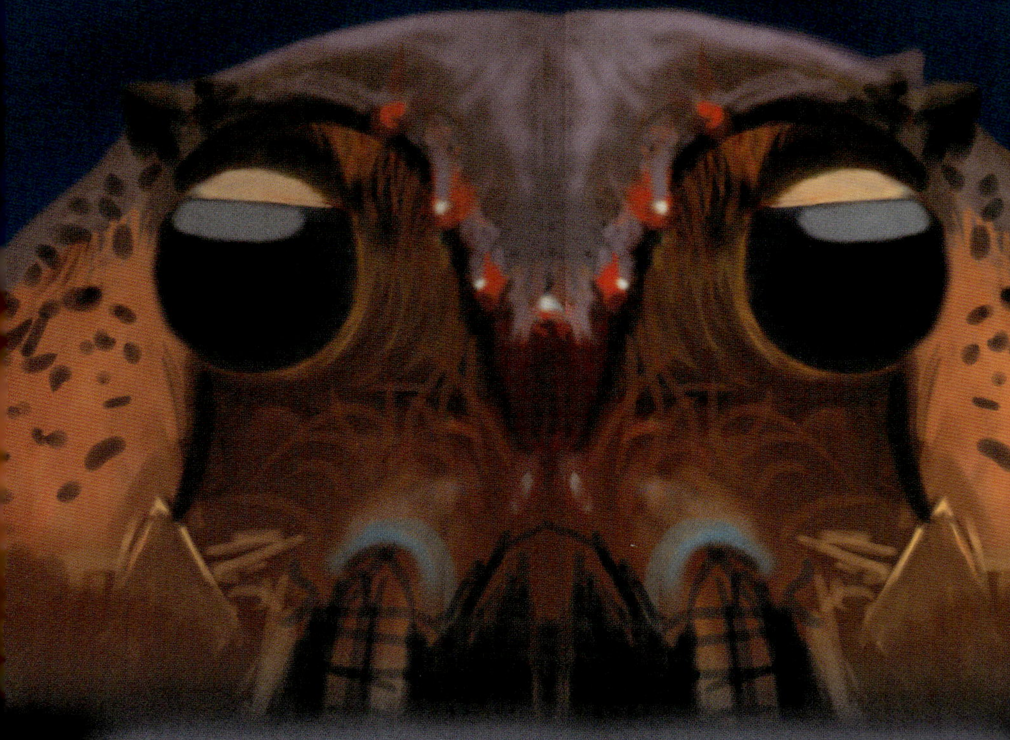

LOBSTER TERMS

KEEPER
A lobster large enough to legally keep.

V-NOTCH TAIL
A female lobster that has bee notched by the Department o Fisheries cannot be kept.

CHICKEN LOBSTER
A keeper lobster that weighs under 1 pound.

CULL
A lobster with only one clau

CRAB EYES

Crabs can't see well. They have a great sense of smell and their antennae can sense motion.

CRAB VOCABULARY

SOOK
A mature female blue crab.

JIMMY
A male blue crab.

WEAPONS

Lobsters have spikes all over their shells. They are armored and ready for battle.

Spikes on the nose.
Spikes on the tail.
Spikes on the knuckles.
3 1/4

FACT
A lobster can curl its tail and cut your fingers or hand.

DEFENSIVE FACT
Lobsters use their claws to defend themselves against fis and other creatures.

MEASURING

QUESTION?
How do you measure a lobster?

ANSWER
With a lobster gauge.

Measure from the eye socket to the end of its head. In n states, the head must be 3-¼ inches long to be a keeper.

ARMOR

A crab has sharp points around its body. Take a good look at a blue crab. Predators can't easily swallow it.

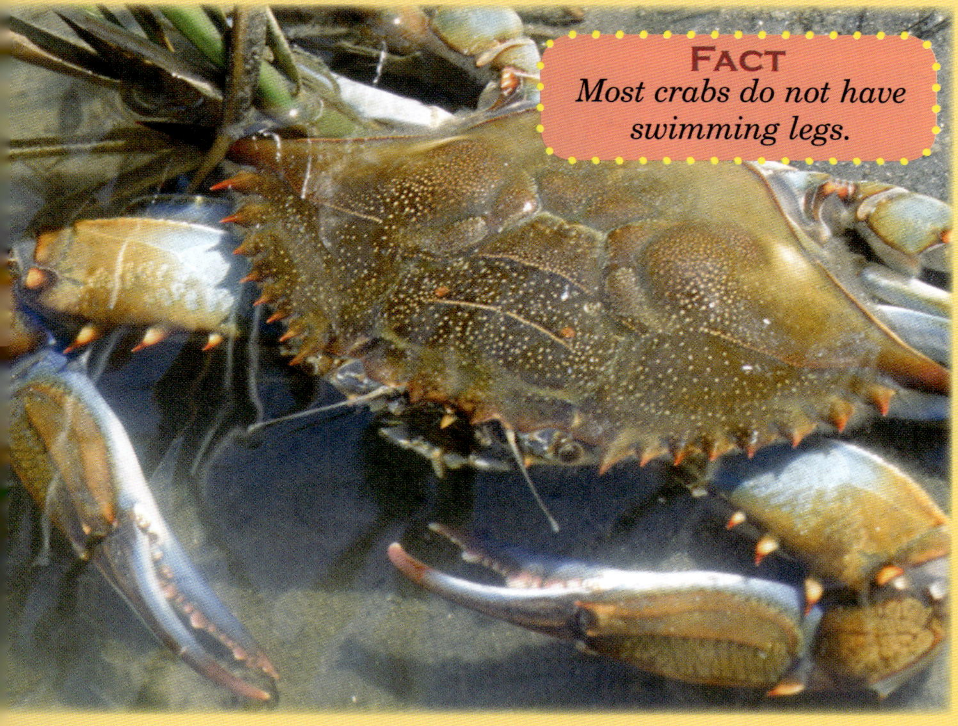

FACT
Most crabs do not have swimming legs.

GAUGE

QUESTION?
Iow do you measure a blue crab?
ANSWER
With a crab gauge.

easure a crab from point to point, from side to side. most states, a crab must be at least five inches long be a keeper.

ARE YOU HUNGRY?

Someone once said, "Everything tastes like chicken, but nothing tastes as good as lobster."

BIG JOE'S
LOBSTER
TODAY'S SPECIALS

Boiled lobster
Baked stuffed lobster
Lobster thermidor
Lobster bisque
Lobster taco
Lobster newburg
Lobster macaroni and cheese

AT BEFORE THE FIGHT

ther people say blue crab is the greatest food on earth.

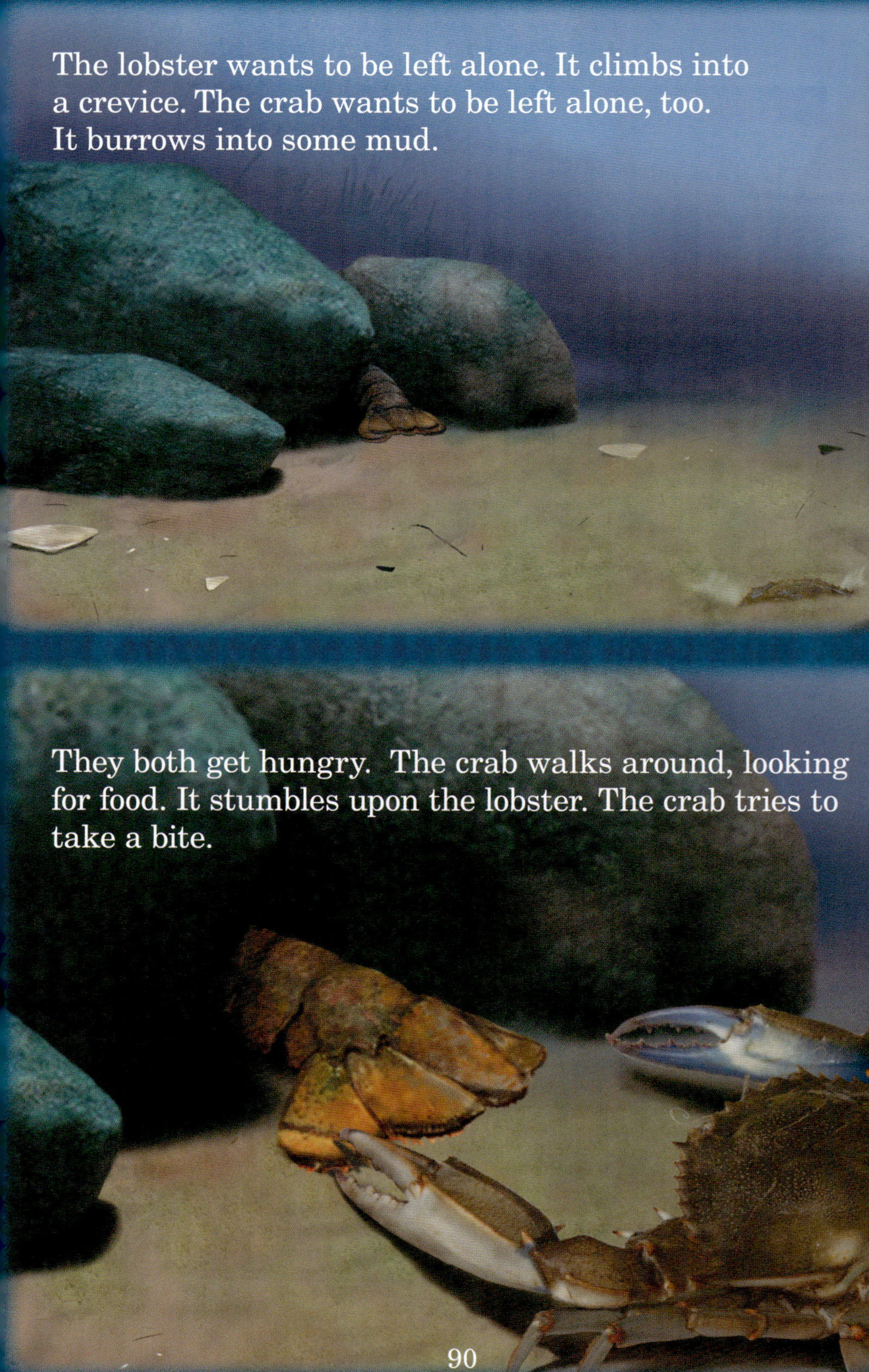

The lobster wants to be left alone. It climbs into a crevice. The crab wants to be left alone, too. It burrows into some mud.

They both get hungry. The crab walks around, looking for food. It stumbles upon the lobster. The crab tries to take a bite.

Whoosh! The lobster flaps its tail and gets away. The crab runs after it. Whoosh! Another flap of its tail, and the lobster gets away. But the lobster is hungry. It walks claws-first at the crab.

The crab flaps its paddle-shaped legs and swims over to the lobster. The lobster is patient. When the crab gets close, the lobster attacks.

The lobster's quick scissor claw grabs the crab by one of its claws. The lobster's crusher claw swings over and *crack*! The lobster damages the crab's claw.

The lobster grabs a couple of legs. Now the crab can't run away. The lobster and the crab fight back and forth. The crab's claws are not strong enough to hurt the lobster.

The lobster moves its crusher claw and bites a chunk off the crab's face.

The crab fills with water from the hole in its shell. This is fatal. The crab slowly stops moving.

The lobster agrees with people. Crabs are delicious.

WHO
WOULD WIN?®

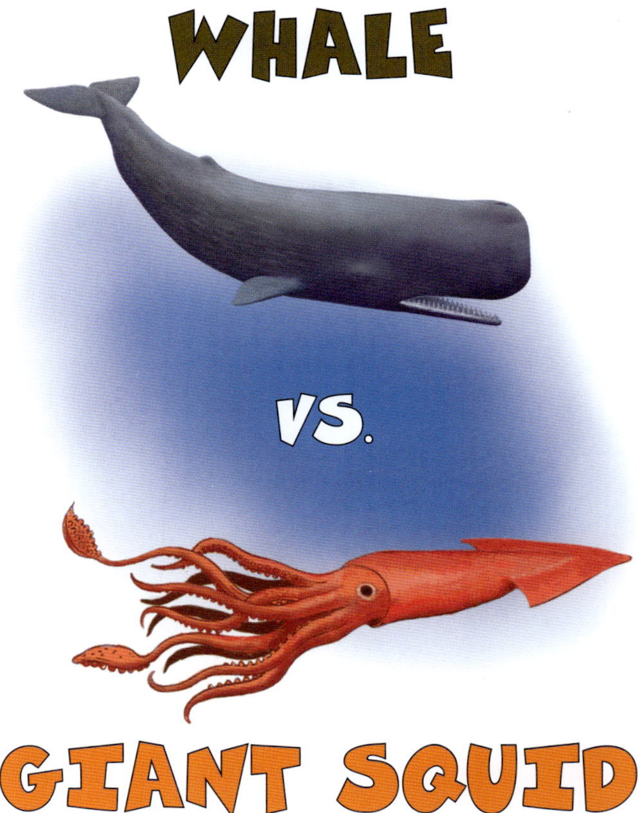
WHALE
VS.
GIANT SQUID

What would happen if a whale swam near a giant squid? They are both carnivores, or meat eaters. What if they had a fight? Who do you think would win?

Scientific Name of Sperm Whale: "Physeter macrocephalus"

Meet the sperm whale.

Big Fact
The blue whale is the largest animal on Earth.

Colorful Fact
Whales have red blood.

Runner-up Fact
The sperm whale can grow to be 60 feet long and weigh 50 tons.

It is one of the world's largest whales. All of the biggest whales are baleen whales, which means they have no teeth. The sperm whale is unusual. It is a big whale that has teeth, but only on its bottom jaw.

his whale looks like a big head with a tail. Its scientific ame means "blower with a big head." It is the largest f all toothed whales. The sperm whale has the largest ead of any animal that has ever lived on Earth.

DID YOU KNOW?
The sperm whale has a blowhole at the front of its head.
LONG FACT
Its head can be 20 feet long.

SCIENTIFIC NAME OF GIANT SQUID: "Architeuthis dux"

Meet the giant squid.

FACT
Squid, octopuses, nautiluses, and cuttlefish are cephalopods.

BONUS FACT
On restaurant menus, squid is often listed by its Italian name, "calamari."

A giant squid is a mollusk. A squid belongs to a group of mollusks called cephalopods. *Cephalopod* means "head fo
A squid looks like a head attached to legs. It has eight legs and two extra feeder arms. The legs have suction cu
The feeder arms have hooks and suction cups on the ends that act like hands.

The giant squid has fins for steering. It propels itself by sucking water into its head and squeezing the water out. A squid works the same way as a jet engine.

GIANT FACT
The largest squid are the giant squid and the colossal squid.

DID YOU KNOW?
A giant squid brain is the size and shape of a small donut.

A giant squid can be 60 feet long and weigh 450 pounds. Most giant squid that have washed up on beaches are 20 to 30 feet long. That's a lot of calamari!

MAMMALS

Whales are mammals. The people reading this book are mammals, too. Here are some other mammals:

SMART FACT
The sperm whale has the largest brain of any animal that has ever lived.

DEFINITION
A mammal is a hairy or furry warm-blooded animal that has a backbone and feeds milk to its young.

MOLLUSKS

Squid are mollusks. Here are examples of other mollusks:

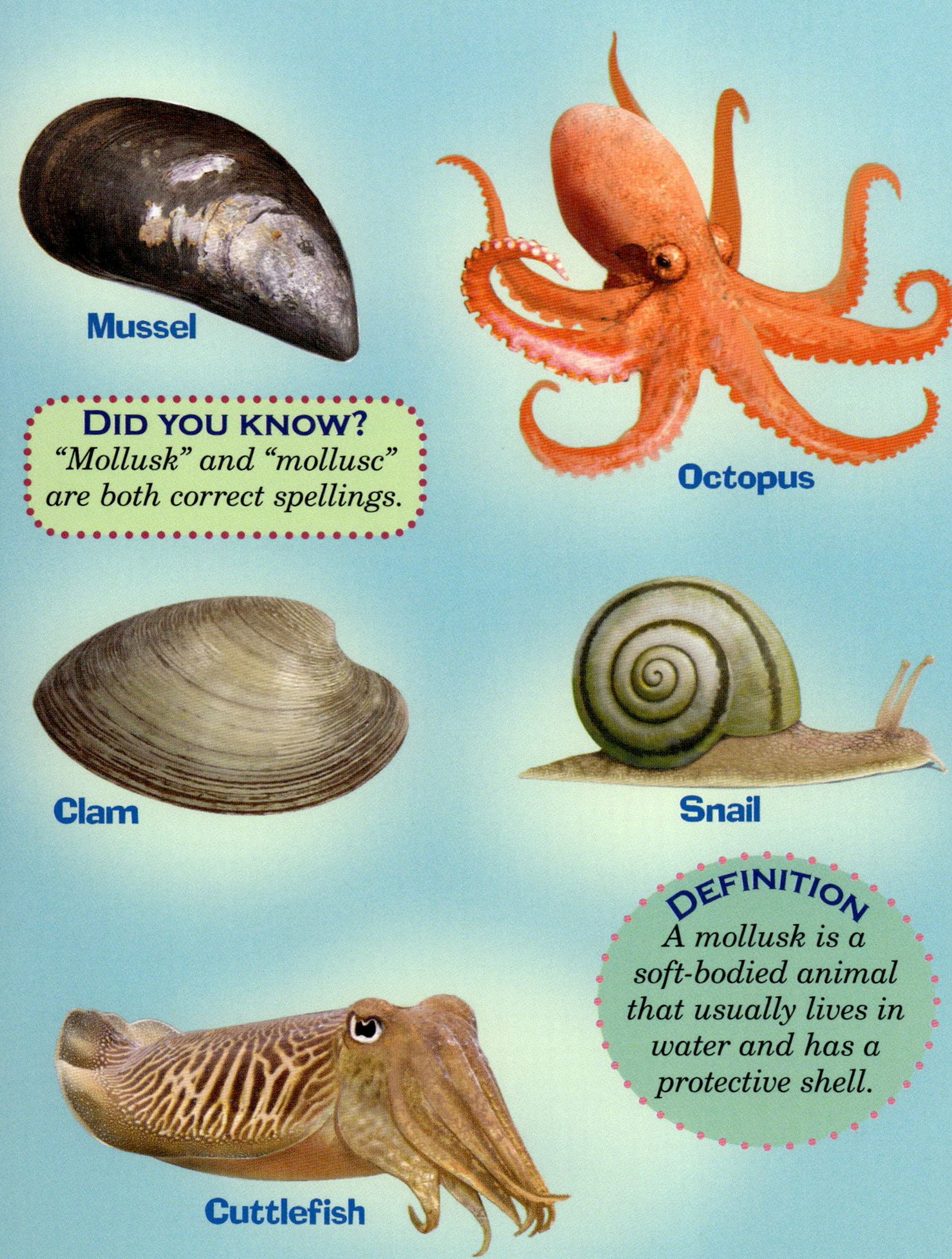

Mussel

Octopus

DID YOU KNOW?
"Mollusk" and "mollusc" are both correct spellings.

Clam

Snail

DEFINITION
A mollusk is a soft-bodied animal that usually lives in water and has a protective shell.

Cuttlefish

EYES

The eye of a sperm whale is only about two inches wide.

Fun Fact
A sperm whale can dive down half a mile. There is hardly any light at that depth.

EYES

Here is a human eyeball. 

Here is a giant squid eyeball in comparison. The giant squid eyeball is the largest eyeball in the world. It is as big as a basketball. Its giant eyeballs allow the squid to see at great depths.

TEETH

The sperm whale has long teeth. The teeth are shaped like sidewalk chalk. Notice that it has no teeth on its upper jaw. When a sperm whale closes its mouth, its bottom teeth fit into the indentations in its upper jaw.

FUN FACT

A sperm whale has 20 to 25 teeth on each side of its lower jaw.

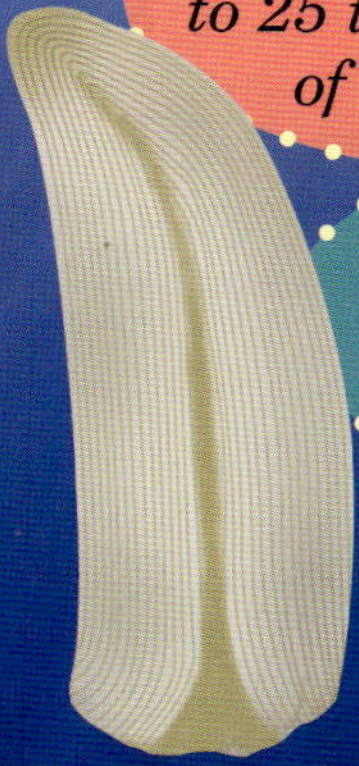

BONUS FACT

You can tell how old a sperm whale is by the layers in its teeth.

DID YOU KNOW?

Whalers used to carve beautiful designs on whale teeth and whale bone. This type of art is called scrimshaw.

BEAK

Between its eight legs and its two feeder arms is the squid's mouth. It does not have teeth. Squid have a beak. It looks like a parrot's beak.

FACT
The tip of a squid's beak is hard and tough, but the lower end is more rubbery.

The beak is made of chitin, a material that is like your fingernails.

TAILS

The tail of a sperm whale can be 16 feet across. Whales have horizontal tails.

DID YOU KNOW?
The winglike tail is also called a fluke.

TRY THIS
Use a measuring tape to mark 16 feet across your classroom. Wow! That is a wide fluke!

Other fluke shapes:

blue whale

humpback whale

sei whale

right whale

FINS

The body of a giant squid is called the mantle or torso. At one end are fins. The giant squid can use its fins to steer. It can also reverse the motion of its fins to swim backward.

FACT
People have seen giant squid jump completely out of the water.

FUN FACT
Squid have three hearts.

BONUS FACT
The squid can also steer itself with its legs.

OIL

Sad but true: Before the discovery of petroleum, whales were a source of oil. It is estimated that 600,000 sperm whales were killed for their oil.

FACT

There are 6 to 8 barrels of oil in the head of a sperm whale.

BONUS FACT

The first time a whale was killed for oil was in 1690. The busiest whaling years were in the 1700s and 1800s.

This is what a typical Nantucket whaling ship looked li
They would often leave port and return four years later.

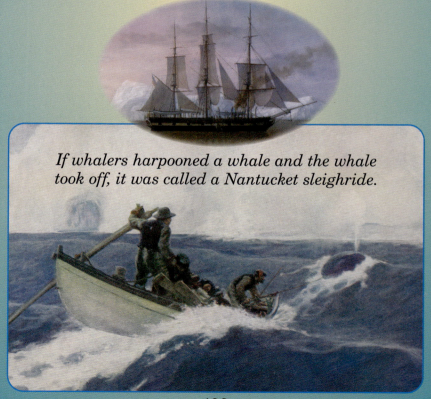

If whalers harpooned a whale and the whale took off, it was called a Nantucket sleighride.

CASH REWARD

No one has ever caught a giant squid and kept it alive. If you ever catch one, it may be worth $1,000,000. Someone will be willing to pay it.

$1,000,000

AWARD

DINNER

Sperm whales eat giant squid, squid, sting rays, octopuses, and fish.

FACT
Some scientists think that wha make such loud underwater clicking sounds that they can shock their food.

FACT
Some squid are called sea arrows.

SUPPER

Giant squid eat fish, shrimps, and other squid. They grab food with their long feeder arms. The feeder arms have sharp spines on the ends. They pull the food into their beaks.

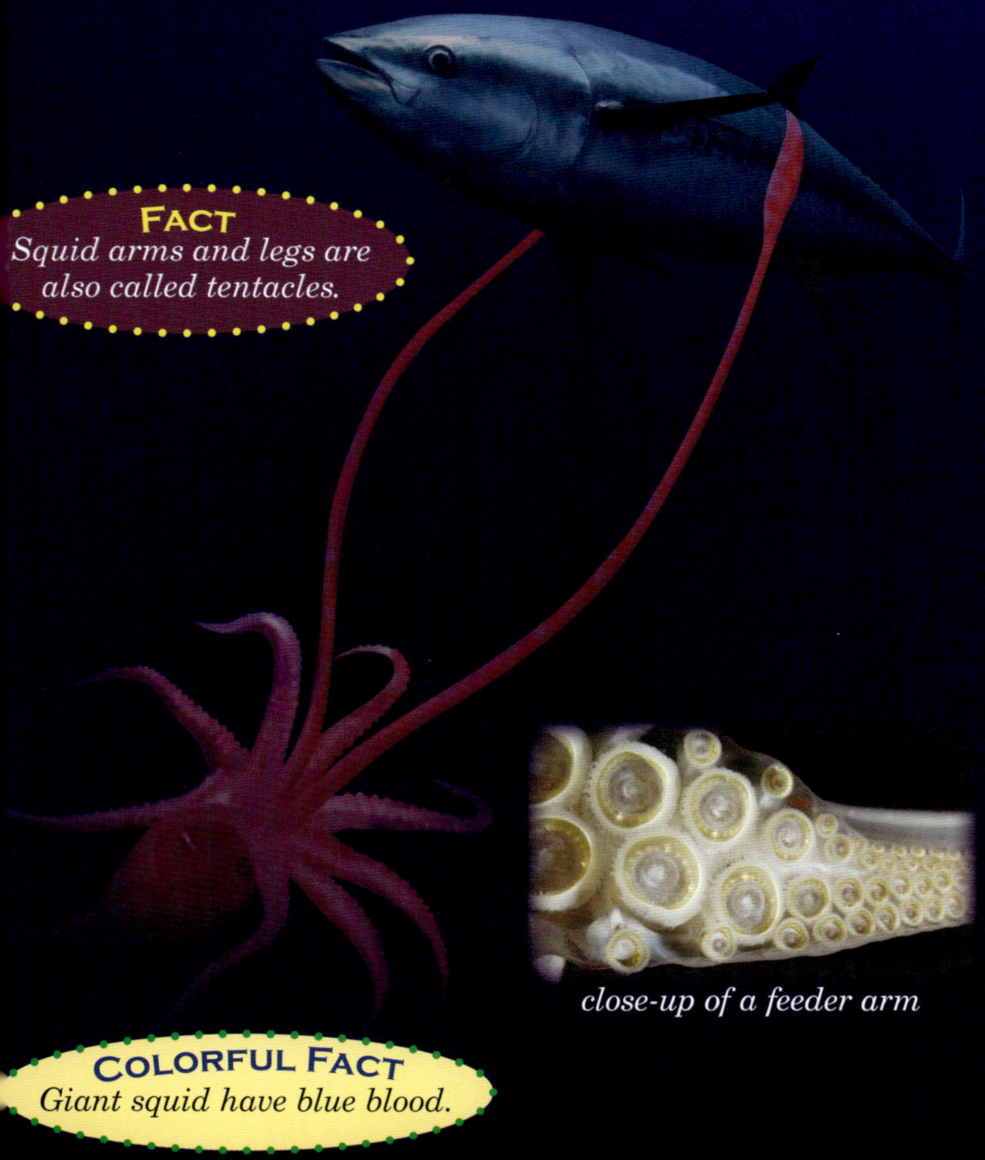

FACT
Squid arms and legs are also called tentacles.

close-up of a feeder arm

COLORFUL FACT
Giant squid have blue blood.

SPEED

A sperm whale can swim 25 miles per hour.

DID YOU KNOW?
A Dall's porpoise can swim faster than 50 miles per hour.

FUN FACT
The fastest fish is the sailfish. It can swim 90 miles per hour.

1/2
MILE

DEPTH

A sperm whale can dive half a mile deep.

AMAZING FACT
Sperm whales can hold their breath for up to two hours. They usually submerge for about 45 minutes.

sperm whale

Empire State Building

ocean floor

SPEED

giant squid can swim 20 miles per hour.

ocean floor

underwater canyon

DEPTH ?

t is not known how far a giant squid can dive. t can dive deeper than a whale. A giant squid is nore agile than a whale. It can change direction uddenly and can swim backward.

FACT
Squid do not need to come up for air.

ECHOLOCATION

In deep water, the whale relies on echolocation to find its way around. It finds its food by bouncing sound signals off its prey. The whale is lucky compared to a squid. A giant squid cannot hear.

DEFINITION

Bouncing sound back from its prey is called echolocation. The whale uses this tc learn where its food is

SOUND FACT

Sonar is the location of objects through sound waves. Bats, whales, shrews, and some birds have sonar. Submarines have sonar, too!

There are many things we don't know about the sperm whale. We don't know why they do not have teeth in their top jaw. We do not know how many get killed by giant squid.

Ve don't know how long a giant squid lives. Some scientists hink it is only three years.

SECRET WEAPON
Squid blow black ink at their attackers. This is called billowing.

DINNER FACT
Some famous chefs use squid ink to make black pasta. It is called squid-ink pasta.

Ve don't know how deep they can dive. We don't know ow many there are. We don't know where they live, but it ppears they prefer deep, colder water. We don't know why o one has been able to catch one alive.

DID YOU KNOW?
There are no known freshwater squid.

FAMOUS WHAL

Moby-Dick is a famous American novel written by Herm Melville. The whale in the story is a giant albino sperm whale. Moby-Dick bit the leg off a captain, who vowed revenge. At the end, the whale rams and sinks the ship.

FUN FACT
Moby-Dick *also became a famous movie.*

The story was based on a real sperm whale that ramme and sank the Nantucket whale ship *Essex*. A nonfiction book was written about the event, called *In the Heart of the Sea* by Nathaniel Philbrick.

FAMOUS LEGEND

For hundreds of years, sailors around the world have been afraid of giant squid. A legend is that they come out of the deep and are so large they can swallow a ship.

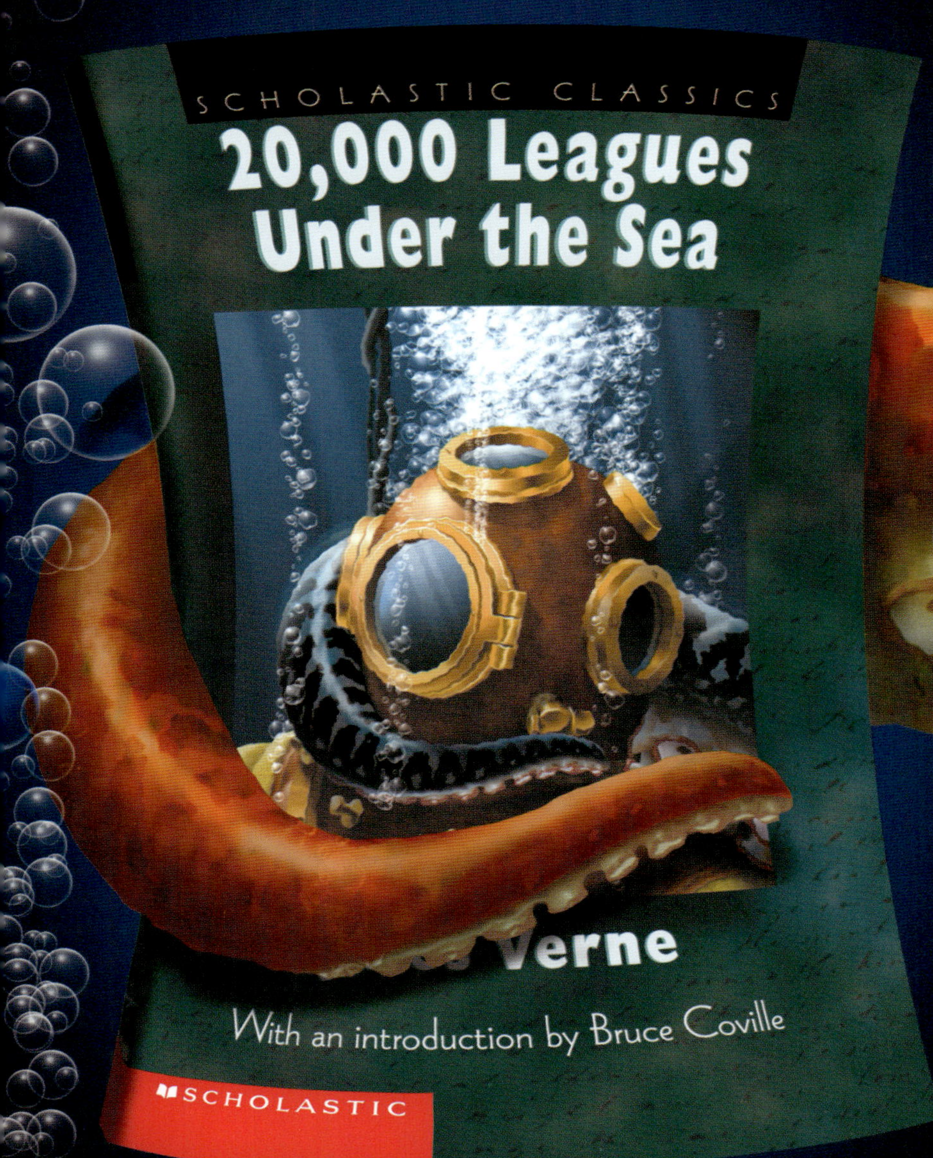

SCHOLASTIC CLASSICS
20,000 Leagues Under the Sea
Verne
With an introduction by Bruce Coville
SCHOLASTIC

Science fiction writer Jules Verne wrote about a giant squid attacking a submarine in a novel called *20,000 Leagues Under the Sea*.

The whale dives. It is looking for food. It sends out sound waves, hoping to find a tasty meal. It senses a few small fish. The whale is hungry. It is looking for a nice giant calamari dinner.

A giant squid is in deep water and out of range.

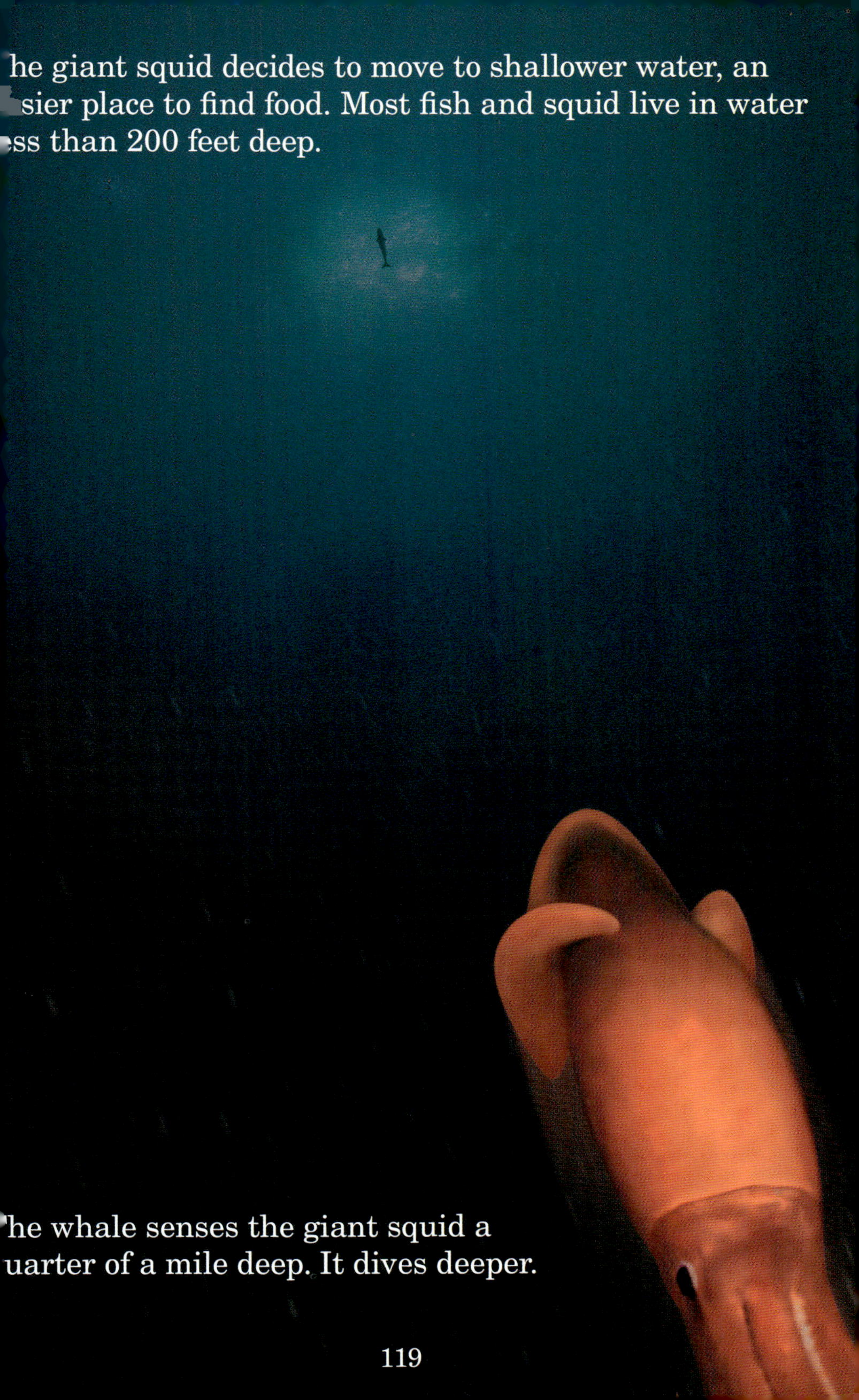

he giant squid decides to move to shallower water, an sier place to find food. Most fish and squid live in water ss than 200 feet deep.

he whale senses the giant squid a uarter of a mile deep. It dives deeper.

The giant squid doesn't notice the whale right away. The whale clicks a few sounds, locates the giant squid, then attacks with its mouth open. The whale grabs a small piece of one of the squid's arms.

The giant squid blows ink in the whale's face, then darts away.

The whale swims after the giant squid. The squid sees the whale and decides to attack first. The squid realizes it is in for a fight. It puts all its legs and feeder arms on the whale. Suction cups and hooks scrape the whale's skin.

The squid tries to hold the whale down until the whale runs out of air. Its plan doesn't work.

The whale maneuvers and bites a chunk of the squid and a few of the squid's arms. A few more bites and the giant squid is in deep trouble.

The whale thinks the giant squid is delicious.

The whale wins, but he has sucker and scratch marks all over his head. That fight hurt!

WHO HAS THE ADVANTAGE? CHECKLIST

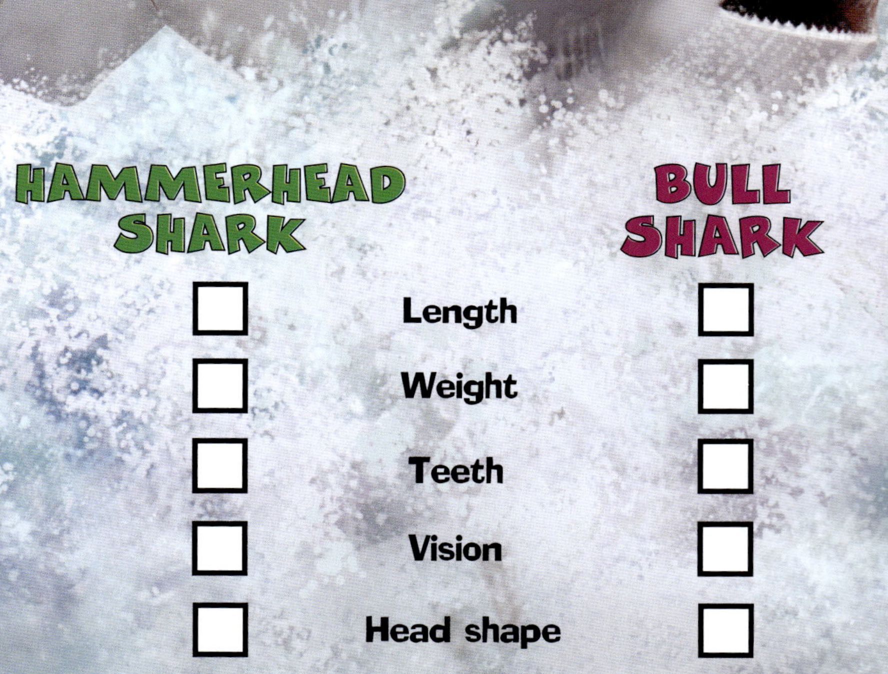

HAMMERHEAD SHARK		BULL SHARK
☐	Length	☐
☐	Weight	☐
☐	Teeth	☐
☐	Vision	☐
☐	Head shape	☐

Author note: This is one way the fight might have ended. How would you write the ending?

WHO HAS THE ADVANTAGE? CHECKLIST

KILLER WHALE		GREAT WHITE SHARK
☐	Breathing	☐
☐	Teeth	☐
☐	Dorsal fin	☐
☐	Size	☐
☐	Tail	☐
☐	Smell	☐
☐	Vision	☐
☐	Family	☐
☐	Intelligence	☐
☐	Speed	☐

Author note: This is one way the fight might have ended. How would you write the ending?

WHO HAS THE ADVANTAGE?

CHECKLIST

Author note: This is one way the fight might have ended. How would you write the ending?

WHO HAS THE ADVANTAGE? CHECKLIST

WHALE		GIANT SQUID
☐	Length	☐
☐	Weight	☐
☐	Brain	☐
☐	Eyes	☐
☐	Teeth	☐
☐	Weapons	☐
☐	Speed	☐

Author note: This is one way the fight might have ended. How would you write the ending?

WHO WOULD WIN?®

UNDERWATER BATTLES